D1617034

NOTORIOUS GRIZZLY BEARS

NOTORIOUS
GRIZZLY
BEARS

W. P. Hubbard
in collaboration with
Seale Harris

SAGE BOOKS
Denver

Library of Congress Catalogue Card Number
60-14583

Sage Books are published by
Alan Swallow, 2679 So. York St., Denver 10, Colo.

To My Father and Mother
who loved the out-of-doors so well

Table of Contents

Table of Illustrations

ACKNOWLEDGMENTS

Many hours were spent by my father and myself in compiling the mass of information contained in this book. Many, many more hours were cheerfully given by good people in helping to verify information picked up through various sources regarding these grizzlies. Without their help much would be lacking.

To these people I give my sincere thanks for a multitude of details and courtesies too numerous to mention.

(A few years ago a fire in a storage shed at the ranch destroyed most of the original notes and records that were taken many years ago, and I extend apologies to any person I should have thanked, whose name may have slipped my memory.)

Durward L. Allen, Dept. Interior, Washington, D. C.;
F. Vernon Bailey, Game & Fish Commission, Santa Fe, New Mexico;
John Barnett, Pryor, Montana;
Floyd Barton, Chester, Montana;
Seth B. Benson, Univ. of California, Berkeley, California;
Mrs. Agnes Caseis, Cedar City, Utah;
Rod Denton, Billings, Montana;
Lon Duncan, Silverton, Colorado;
Marshall Edson, Game & Fish Commission, Boise, Idaho;
W. L. Flinn, Game & Fish Commission, Denver, Colorado;
Charles Foley, San Francisco, California;
Alys Freeze, Public Library, Denver, Colorado;
Ed Francis, Anchorage, Alaska;
James E. Grasse, Game & Fish Commission, Cheyenne, Wyoming;
Pete Henry, Blackfoot, Idaho;
Paul Hickie, Dept. Interior, Washington, D. C.;
N. W. Hosley, Dept. Interior, Washington, D. C.;
Remington Kellog, Smithsonian Institution, Washington, D. C.;
R. E. Kenoffel, Firefly Springs, Idaho.
Harry Kincaid, Helena, Montana;
James Lake, Troy, Montana;
John Larrick, Cedar City, Utah;

J. Burton Lauckhart, Game & Fish Commission, Seattle, Washington;
Tom Lloyd, Nass Bay, British Columbia;
Juan Martinez, Redding, California;
Ford Ulysses McCorkle, Casper, Wyoming;
Caleb Myres, Missoula, Montana;
Allen R. Ottley, State Library, Sacramento, California;
George Padget, Game & Fish Commission, Cheyenne, Wyoming;
Flora M. Reese, Blackfoot, Montana;
George W. Reynolds, Game & Fish Commission, Cheyenne, Wyoming;
Ed Rowe, Santa Fe, New Mexico;
Carl Schroder, Pryor, Montana;
F. M. Setzler, Smithsonian Institution, Washington, D. C.
Mrs. Gertrude Springs, Helena, Montana;
Janet Sterling, Canon City, Colorado;
M. W. Sterling, Smithsonian Institution, Washington, D. C.;
Arthur Svihla, Univ. of Washington, Seattle, Washington;
Glenn Thompson, Santa Ana, California;
Carma R. Zimmerman, State Library, Sacramento, California.

In addition to these individuals, my sincere thanks and acknowledgments are due the following authors and publishers for permission to quote from their works.

Russell Annabel and *Sports Afield* magazine, for quotes from "Grizzlies Are Such Interesting Neighbors" and other extracts; AP and the *Denver Post* for news items; AP and *Rocky Mountain News* for news items; Walter Colton for quotes from *Three Years in California;* the *Empire Magazine* and its editor, H. Ray Baker, and the *Denver Post* for several story quotes; Cory Ford and The Curtis Publishing Company, for quotes by the author in his article "Biggest Bear On Earth," in the *Saturday Evening Post;* Frank C. Hibben and *True Magazine* for quotes from "One Bite Is Enough"; Theodore H. Hittell and C. Scribner's Sons for quotes from *The Adventures of James Capen Adams;* H. T. Liliencrantz and *Western Horseman* magazine for quotes from his articles and other information he so kindly sent me; C. Hart Merriam, and U. S. Government Printing Office for facts and statistics; The Smithsonian Institution for various information given; The Fish & Game Commissions of the eleven western states for statistics and information given; W. M. Rush and Halcyon House for quotes; the *Sacramento Bee* and McClatchy Newspaper Service for news items; the *Daily Alta California* for news items; the *Sacramento Daily Union* for news items; the *San Diego Union* for news items; the *Elgin Bul-*

letin for news items; James Willard Schultz and Grossett & Dunlap for quotes in *Lone Bull's Mistake;* Janet Sterling and the *Denver Post* for her article "Old Mose"; W. H. Wright and C. Scribner's Sons for various quotes.

Especial thanks are due to Charles Coxe, who assisted with a multitude of corrections in my longhand version; to my many Indian friends among the Blackfeet Indians who aided so much on many matters; to the many unknown cowboys, trappers, guides, and packers, whose tales around the campfire or on the trail built up the background material in my mind; and finally, my thanks to my collaborator Seale Harris whose patience and assistance put the finishing touches on this book.

W.P.H.

A Few Words about the Grizzly Population

In the July, 1959, issue of *Wyoming Wildlife Magazine*, Mr. George W. Reynolds, Chief of the Information and Education Department of the Wyoming Game and Fish Commission, wrote the following article entitled "The Silver Ghost." Mr. Reynolds' article is a grim warning of what can happen to the grizzly bear, as has already happened to our passenger pigeon. Let us hope that this article will be the start of a protective movement to save these magnificent animals from extinction, and that other states having a grizzly population will follow Wyoming's start at protecting them.

Sportsmen through the nation should let it be known that they back any right movement for the protection of the grizzly.

Mr. George Padget, editor of *Wyoming Wildlife Magazine*, and Mr. Reynolds are both sportsmen whose interests in wildlife conservation run far beyond that of their employment with the Wyoming Game and Fish Commission. It was from them permission was secured to reprint the entire article as follows:

THE SILVER GHOST

One day we may awake to find that the Silver Ghost is just that—a ghostly memory, a shade that exists only in museums, on fading photographs and in our twinging conscience.

Yes, we're going to lose our grizzly bears unless we do something to protect them. That's the opinion of wildlife men who know the grizzly, who have seen him forced farther and farther back into the high country and who have seen his numbers cut a third in a single decade.

In just ten years' time grizzlies have dropped from an estimated 1,265 in the entire 48 states to 844. Men who are familiar with these figures believe that 844 is an overly-generous estimate.

In 1956 Dave Condon, Chief Naturalist for Yellowstone National Park, reported that Montana estimated it had about 440 grizzlies, more than all the rest of the states combined.

"Today," Condon said, "in the United States he is reported from Colorado's San Juan Mountains, where a few are reported to remain; Washington, which says it may have one or more; Idaho, with probably 50 to 60; Wyoming with an estimated 25 to 50; Montana's liberally estimated population and those found in Grand Teton, Glacier, and Yellowstone national parks."

Conversations with people who have direct interests in grizzlies bear out Condon's belief that the figures are high. A search of the San Juans a few years ago turned up reports of grizzlies, but no actual sightings, and in Idaho there are varying opinions over grizzly numbers in that state. The estimate for Yellowstone Park is 120 to 180. The 25 to 50 grizzlies which are estimated to be in Wyoming range in Teton and Park counties in the rugged, wild country bordering Yellowstone Park. In a sense, they are part of the same population as the grizzlies in the park. Yellowstone's grizzly numbers have shown no increase in recent years. This is because a few cross the park line each year seeking new range. It is these migrants which have helped sustain Wyoming's gradually dwindling grizzly population.

Writing in *Wyoming Wildlife* in February, 1955, Lester Bagley (State Game and Fish Commissioner at that time) summed up the bear situation this way:

"There are an estimated fifty grizzly bear left in Wyoming. Present laws and regulations permit approximately 85,000 persons each year to hunt for these animals—1,700 possible hunters for each grizzly as compared to a possible 74 hunters for each one of our 1,120 black bear.

"In addition to sport hunters, bear on livestock range are confronted by the effective baits and rifles of professional predator control men.

"Even in national parks bears do not enjoy complete protection. In these areas they must either be docile enough to get along with thousands of sight-seers from cities or else face deportation or death before the firing squad. Reports indicate that grizzlies are not doing well under these circumstances.

"The past four years have seen our grizzly population cut almost in half. In five years black bear numbers have been reduced almost fifty percent.

"We must soon decide whether we wish to exterminate bear because of their role as possible and actual livestock predators or whether we wish to manage them in select areas in controlled numbers as a native game animal worth preserving.

"Another year or two of indecision and there will be no decision left to make."

A decision is being made. At its November 1958 meeting the Wyoming Game and Fish Commission passed a minute with a view to protecting grizzlies on remote, non-livestock ranges. The Commission will consider closure of grizzly bear hunting in 1960 in areas not affecting stock operations.

Exactly which areas will be considered for closure had not been definitely decided at the time of this writing. It can be assumed the areas will be within 100 air miles of the park's boundary and will be planned to exclude areas of heavy stock use.

Just what the action of the commission will be is going to be determined by reaction of the public and of those stockmen whose operations are adjacent to proposed grizzly no-hunting areas.

In the meantime, there will likely be an open season this fall. The casual bear hunter—the elk or deer hunter with a bear tag on his license—who chances onto a grizzly might think twice before squeezing the trigger. What he's killing may not be just a bear; it could be the very last mature sow or bear grizzly within 20 or 30 miles.

With proper protection for the magnificent grizzly, Wyoming can always be proud that it acted soon enough.

—George W. Reynolds

14

Introduction

Only a few authentic books and articles have been written portraying the grizzly bear the noble animal that he is. Their authors have been men who hunted, photographed, and, in most cases, made a study of the great bears for years, or were writers who sought out reliable information. No words can speak too highly of their work and effort in rectifying the slanderous charges which have been made intentionally or unintentionally against the grizzly. On the other hand, considerable fiction has been written about them, very little of which is factual or accurately describes their true character and habits. In the early days the majority of grizzly stories did nothing but create conflicting opinion; these, in time, caused the grizzly to suffer almost to the point of extinction.

Throughout the past thirty-four years, I have hunted in the United States, Mexico, Alaska, and Canada. In that time I have killed five grizzlies, three of them in a most unexpected manner, while working for a pack outfit in northern British Columbia. While in that northern country, and during the years spent working for various cow outfits and professional guides as a packer and horse-wrangler from Alaska to Old Mexico, it has been my good fortune to watch a fair number of grizzlies in their natural habitat. During my rambles, many old-timers' trails have been crossed—men who have hunted and observed grizzlies for years. From them I gained much additional and reliable information.

My father, the late Charles Price Hubbard, began collecting data on outlaw grizzlies in 1914. After his passing in 1925, I took up the work. Some of the tales heard were true, others highly exaggerated or purely mythological. Over a period of thirty-four years, I have been able to gain full, authentic accounts of the lives of but a few livestock-killing grizzlies. Three of these grizzlies were what are sometimes referred to as color freaks, or pintos. Eighteen others were outlaw livestock killers with bounties on their heads, but the variation in the accounts of their lives and deeds were so numerous and conflicting that it was impossible to authenticate them.

Along with my father's notes, additional information about the outlaw grizzlies usually came to me from talks with old-time stockmen. After that came painstaking searching of available aged livestock association records, and talks with persons mentioned in the records as having knowledge of the bears under investigation. Leads and information were also acquired from old-time bear hunters, reliable books, state libraries, early day newspaper accounts and historical documents. From this mass of information, although a few inaccuracies may have unknowingly crept in, I have been able to set forth in this book the detailed histories of six stock-killing grizzlies that roamed the mountains and range lands of the western United States.

However grizzlies were not all the same.

With the continuous influx of civilization on his range, the grizzly's food supply dwindled. These bears, like all other wild animals, followed God's given law of self preservation. Therefore, with the passing of much of his natural food supply, and the coming of domestic stock, the grizzly turned to the latter for food on rare occasions. A few of them became persistent livestock killers, or "outlaws," in the eyes of some stockmen.

What actually brought that name upon them, as well as the assumed belief that all grizzlies were wanton destroyers of domestic stock because of the acts of a few of their kind, is the fact they hurt "man's pocketbook" when they killed his domestic animals.

Man does not call a robin a wanton killer when a robin takes a worm from his ground for food.

A grizzly, or any other wild animal, is no more a wanton killer, when it slays a domestic or wild animal to satisfy its hunger so that it can continue its life's existence, than is a robin, when it pulls a worm from the ground for its food to continue its life's existence.

Think it over!

—W. P. Hubbard

The Grizzly Bears

Early History

The English-speaking history of the grizzly bear begins on April 29, 1805, on the banks of the upper Missouri River near the mouth of the Yellowstone River, in what is now the state of Montana. On this day, Captain Meriwether Lewis, of the Lewis and Clark Expedition, met one of these animals for the first time. Prior to that meeting, rumors of a huge bear living in the wilderness west of the Mississippi River, differing from the bears known in the eastern states, came back to civilization with returning explorers and trappers, but there was no authentic information about them.

Lewis and Clark were the first to enter in their journals full accounts of their various encounters with these animals, and to make inquiries about them among the Indians of the regions where they were found. About forty-five years after their expedition their field notes were still the chief source of information pertaining to the grizzly.

From other explorers, hunters, fur traders, trappers, and the following horde of pioneers who settled the West, came a large amount of knowledge gained about the grizzly and other species of bear they encountered.

Before the white man invaded the West, the grizzly, when occasionally attacked by Indians using arrows, knives, spears, and clubs, defended himself with a success that was astounding. Indians feared the grizzly above all animals and seldom hunted them. Among the Blackfeet Indians, to kill a grizzly was considered as brave a deed as killing an enemy.

The explorers, trappers, and settlers, with their longbarreled, smoothbore guns, presented something new to the grizzly—the experience of being injured from a long distance. Regardless of the smoothbore gun, the bears continued to charge when injured, surprised, or attacked. To this day, under similar circumstances, they will charge against our modern, high powered rifles. As time went on and more pioneers invaded their domain, and as their encounters with men became more frequent, they became wary. With the continuous flow of settlers, who were equipped with more effective rifled barreled guns, their respect for man increased to the point of hesitant caution.

In time the human scent struck a stern warning to the grizzly, and to this day, in most cases and if possible, he will try to move away unseen before the human arrives. If seen before he can escape, then he usually tries to depart in a dignified manner to save face, for he is not a coward.

While generalities apply most of the time to the grizzly, their routine is constantly open to exception. Aroused, they are formidable opponents. They are most dangerous when come upon at kills, or caches, or with their young, or surprised at close quarters, or cornered (or think they are). Under any of these circumstances they will usually charge their antagonist with wild, rushing bounds, sometimes covering ten to twelve feet at a clip. Nothing but death will stop them in their mad fury.

The coming of livestock, continually being hunted by settlers, professional hunters, and trappers, continuous improvement of firearms, and lack of adequate game laws to protect them are the chief factors contributing to the grizzlies' rapid destruction. Before long they were eliminated from much of their once vast domain, and by 1915 they were nearing extinction.

Classification

About the first of the century, naturalists made a classification of bears. Dr. C. Hart Merriam made the first acknowledged classification of the North American bears. They were placed in five well-marked, specific groups or types. Since this book deals only with the grizzly bear, only Dr. Merriam's classification of the grizzly is given. He states:

The Grizzly Bears (including the Barren Ground Bear) may be separated into four more or less well-marked forms as follows:

A. The True Grizzly, Ursus Horribilis Ord, from the northern Rocky Mountains.[1]
B. The Sonora Grizzly, Ursus Horribilis Horriaeus Baird, probably only a subspecies.
C. The North Sound Alaskan Grizzly, probably another subspecies.
D. The very distinct Barren Ground Bear, Ursus Richardsoni Mayne Reid. Whether or not the large grizzly from Southern California deserves subspecific separation from the Sonora animal (Horriaeus) has not been determined.

Since Dr. Merriam's classification, naturalists and scientists have learned more about these bears, and have given them a broader scope of classification as to range. They are now classed as the northern grizzly, Ursus Horribilis, inhabiting the Rockies westward to the Pacific, and from Utah to the interior of British Columbia; the southern, or Sonoran, grizzly, U. h. Horriaeus, inhabiting the southern Rockies from Colorado to Arizona; and the California grizzly, U. h. Californius, now extinct, which was found in central and southern California.

Because of this wide range, let it be understood that in this book all accounts and statements made, unless specified otherwise, pertain only to grizzlies in the areas in which they are mentioned. Because of the environment in which they live, their behavior and habits vary in individuals and in different sections of the country.

Other types of grizzly and other bears, will be discussed only for comparison and interest. Grizzlies should not be confused with our common black, brown, and cinnamon bears.

Range

In the United States, the grizzly's range of old covered the entire area from the western Dakotas southward to western

---

[1]Because the True Grizzly was first encountered in the northern Rocky Mountain region by Lewis and Clark. he is scientifically classified from that area. However, the True Grizzly's range is spread over many of our western states.

Texas and westward to the Pacific. Since 1930, no wild grizzlies have been seen, or known to exist, in Oregon, Nevada, Utah, New Mexico, or Arizona. None has lived in California, in a wild state, since 1922.

No known, reliable estimate of the grizzly population was ever made in the early days. However, in later years through various government sources, several estimates were made. From the United States Department of the Interior, Fish and Wildlife Service, in a letter dated September 2, 1948, the following information was obtained on this subject:

So far as we know there are no real estimates of grizzly bears in the United States prior to 1922. Probably the best account of early numbers is given in Seaton's "Lives of Game Animals," Volume II, Part 1, pages 5 to 75. However, his information is based on numbers seen on various trips and in given lengths of time. The first real estimate of which we know was made by Dr. C. H. Merriam in 1922. At that time he estimated there were 800 grizzlies in the United States, chiefly in Wyoming, Montana and Colorado. A more careful check in 1937 gave an estimate of 1,100 for the United States which showed that Merriam must have been low on his figure. In 1937 it was felt that there must have been at least 2,000 grizzlies in 1922.

The following census, taken in 1946 and 1952 by the U. S. Fish and Wildlife Service, places the grizzly population within the bounds of the United States as listed below. These bears were known to be living at those times within the bounds of our national parks and monuments, Indian reservations, national and state forests, and federal, state, and private lands.

State	1946	1952
Washington	3	0
Idaho	60	69
Colorado	26	32
Montana	772	758
Wyoming	487	349
	1348	1208

This shows a total of 1348 grizzlies for 1946 against a total of 1208 for 1952, a decrease of 140 grizzlies in 6 years, or better than ten percent.

Since 1954, an average of one grizzly a year has been killed in Washington. Ten per year have been killed by hunters in Wyoming. No actual sightings of grizzlies have been made in the past several years in Colorado, but from evidence of their existence it is estimated there are seventeen grizzlies in that state.

Information received in the fall of 1959 from the Game and Fish Commissions of these states estimate, from sightings of grizzlies and other evidence of their existence, that their respective grizzly population, including national parks and monuments, Indian reservations, national and state forests, and federal, state, and private lands, is:

State	1959
Washington	10
Idaho	49
Colorado	17
Montana	550
Wyoming	230
	856

This total compared with the 1952 total shows a decrease of 352 grizzlies, a depletion of one-fourth of the grizzly population in only seven years. One can readily see that these great bears are swiftly on the decline and within another few years, unless something is done quickly to protect them, they will be completely annihilated.

Pelage and Character

Coloration

Research confirms that the color of the grizzly conforms with no known law of coloration. I have seen grizzlies in all shades of color, ranging from almost jet black through the browns and creams to practically white. However, I have never seen, heard, or read of an albino grizzly. Bears with large white markings are referred to as pintos, or color freaks. One rarely finds two grizzlies of the same color. It is not uncommon to see an old she-bear with three cubs, each of a different color; for example, one a dark brown, verging almost upon black, a second of light buff, and the third almost white, or white as far back as the shoulders. I have seen only one litter of cubs that were all the same color as their mother. The reason for this great variety of color is unknown. It is, however, an indisputable fact, and typical of the species throughout its range.

Probably due to this extreme range of coloring, hunters and trappers have continuously maintained that there are many different kinds of grizzlies throughout the western states, and in the Rocky Mountain area in particular. The varieties of grizzlies have been termed the roach-back, silver-tip, bald-face, range-bear, and, occasionally, the real-bear. This last name was probably picked up from the Blackfeet Indians, whose country covered most of Montana, and who referred to the grizzly as real-bear. Bears in general were called sticky-mouths by the Blackfeet.

The grizzlies ranging east of, and in, the Rocky Mountain areas of Wyoming, Colorado, and northern New Mexico are the smallest of their species. Their coloring is usually light, that is, of whitish hue.

In Wyoming, the grizzlies' coloring runs from medium brown to lightish-brown to buffish-white, the hair on their entire head being of a light buff color. They are sometimes referred to as "bald-faced" grizzlies. On one occasion, late one evening in the Wind River Mountains of Wyoming, I watched a grizzly that was unusually light in color, appearing in the twilight to be almost silvery white over her entire body. Both her cubs appeared to be deep brown.

Several years ago, Charlie Bragg and I were working for the old Sunset cow outfit, which was located on the Gros Ventre River in the eastern foothills of the Gros Ventre Mountains in Wyoming. While there we heard about a black bear, with decided white markings, that ranged in the mountains above the ranch. On three occasions riders told of seeing the bear in the vicinity of one of the outfit's line camps. Later in the summer a party of vacationers and their guides told us of seeing such a bear. All described it as an adult with one white spot on the neck that ran back over the shoulder and another that covered part of one side, rump, and leg.

When the fall roundup ended, we packed in to the line camp, which was about the center of the bear's known range. The camp was at the end of a narrow valley surrounded by boulder canyons, with both standing and fallen timber, and a series of small meadows—typical bear country.

We started hunting on foot the morning after our arrival, as the terrain was too rough for horses. At a "rubbing post" we happened upon, we found black and brown bear fur caught in the bark and on the ground around the base of the post. One patch contained a good portion of white hair. This gave us encouragement, but we could not find the pinto.

According to all the laws of nature, snakes at that time of year should have denned up for the winter. Having taken such for granted, the yell I let out on our way back to camp has never been duplicated. A rattler hit me on the inside of my right leg. The snake was a big devil, and although first aid was given, the damage was done. After that, Charlie did all the hunting while I remained in camp waiting for the swelling in the leg to go down.

A few days later the first heavy snowstorm of the season drove us down to low country. We never saw the pinto alive.

The bear changed his range. Three years later, in 1932, on the other side of the mountains and about eighteen miles from where

23

we had hunted, it was killed by Thelma Corder of Seattle, Washington, while on an elk hunt with her husband. The bear was a big male, about eight years old. His white markings were as described. His hide was made into an open-mouth rug. Charlie and I saw it at the taxidermist's. This bear is the last pinto of which I know.

I have a grizzly rug, the bear having been shot by my father in 1920 on Chichagof Island, Alaska, that measures ten feet and one-half inch from the tip of its nose to the tip of its tail. The bear weighed 1015 pounds. In color it is dark gray, except for a black stripe about eight inches wide which runs from the center of the head down the middle of the back, with another black stripe running from one fore paw up the leg, over the shoulder and down the other fore leg to the paw. The stripes form a decided cross against the rest of his grayish, silver-tipped pelage. At one time my father owned the pelt of a grizzly killed in Mexico in 1899. It was a liver-cocoa brown color tinged and grizzlied with a yellowish tan.

Lewis and Clark, in their journals, mentioned the grizzlies' coloring, and refer to them as "gray, white, brown, and varigated" bear. They put down at some length their own conclusions and the opinions of the Indians in regard to the bearing of these color variations. In this respect there is no difference in their time and the present.

Dr. William T. Hornaday, of the New York Zoological Society, summed up the question of grizzly coloring in a letter to one of his friends who asked about their true color: "Regarding the color of the grizzly, it remains today just as Lewis and Clark found it a century ago. . . . So far as I can judge, the color of the grizzly conforms to no known law of coloration."

Weight

A safe estimate of the average weight of adult grizzlies in our western states would be about eight hundred and fifty pounds. This conclusion results from a careful check on grizzlies killed and weighed by numerous hunters, trappers, and old-time bear men.

Nevertheless, there are exceptions. Several outlaw grizzlies investigated were known to have weighed over one thousand pounds.

Matings and Cubs

Grizzlies mate every second or third year. On the average a grizzly has either two or three cubs to a litter, usually only two. Once I saw a grizzly with four cubs, and on three occasions one with but one. I have seen a good many with two, and several with three.

When the cubs are born, they are about nine inches long and weigh from one and a half to two pounds. They are usually born in January or February, but the she-bear does not bring them out of the den until April or May. A female will keep her cubs with her through the first winter after their birth and occasionally the second.

The mating time of these bears throughout the northwest runs according to locality, from about the middle of June until about the first of August. I cannot say whether individual males and females deliberately hunt each other out during the mating season, pair off and stay together for a few weeks, or whether they meet by chance and separate quickly. The latter is the more credible.

Lone Travelers

Only once have I seen adult grizzlies traveling together for any length of time. On numerous occasions I have seen them pay no heed to another's presence when they came close, other than acting as if surprised at the meeting, although in some instances they were in plain sight and aware of each other's presence for a long time.

I once watched a big male unexpectedly come upon an old she with two cubs that were digging skunk-cabbage roots in a marshy clearing. At sight of them the male paused, circled the clearing, and continued on his way. The old lady just kept up her low, growling conversation with her cubs—a general characteristic of a female with young. The three of them never stopped their digging.

The one time I saw adult grizzlies together for any length of time was not in their mating season. It was in late October in the rough country south of Glacier National Park. Both were big, brownish fellows. I saw their tracks together for over a month, and watched them at various times during that period. Early one morning, for no apparent reason, they left the bog where they were feeding and took off fast up a river course. I watched them from a ridge as long as I could. When last seen through my field glasses, they were dropping behind the top of a knoll.

Often one grizzly's trail crosses that of others, since two, three, and more bears may roam the same district. There is no question that grizzlies sometimes engage in fights over territory or for the possession of a female, but fights are rare, and in most cases the age-old "eternal triangle" is the probable cause.

The grizzly will chase away and even kill our common bears if it comes in contact with them. However, anyone who has seen the agility with which a black, brown, or cinnamon bear will take to a tree if a grizzly happens along, knows they will never allow themselves to be killed if they can avoid the meeting in time.

When salmon are battling upstream to spawn, I have observed adults come down the same trail together to fish and occasionally leave together for short distances. Usually they left separately and in different directions.

Denning Up

Cub bears frequently den together the first winter they are on their own, but after that they break up and den alone. Adult bears den singly. The male hibernates earlier than the female and comes out of hibernation earlier.

The grizzly likes to den in high country, near, at, or above timberline. Sometimes they return to the same den for several years in succession. Their dens are most often located on northern slopes, or in the shaded recesses of narrow canyons, or deep ravines. This is due to the fact that northern slopes and such locations receive less sun and consequently the bears are out of hibernation before melting snow water soaks the den. In the colder parts of Alaska and Canada, old bear men assure me that grizzlies hibernate in October, while those in warmer climates along the Alaskan coast may remain out until late November or early December. In the western states, where climate conditions are milder, they usually den up in November or December, coming out in late April or early May. In the warmer climates of the southwest, they are known to come out as early as late February or mid-March.

They most often den in natural caves and close the entrance with brush and limbs to keep out the snow and cold. Sometimes they will enlarge a small opening in a bank or dig back in a crevice. Once I found a den well concealed and sheltered under a jumble of windfalls that lay criss-crossed so heavily that the top of the den was completely covered with dead trees, limbs, and creeping brambles. At times a bear will dig his own den under a log or overhanging ledge of rock, under or beside the roots of a fallen or standing tree. In Montana, I saw such a den under the base of a windfall that had wedged itself between two boulders. The den was between the boulders and had the tree for a roof. This den measured seven feet in diameter by five feet four inches high. Where several roots grew close together, the bear had chewed one off to make an entrance. Then it had dug the den into the space between the boulders and roots. Its floor was covered with dead grass and shreds of bark and leaves.

In early spring, by back tracking fresh bear tracks in the snow, I have found several dens in rocky caves and pockets high in the mountains.

Forest Ranger W. M. Rush, in his book, *Wild Animals of the Rockies*, tells of finding a den equipped with what one might call a bench-like bed. He said:

One October morning after a new fall of snow, I came upon fresh tracks of a big black bear on a steep, forested hillside. At that time of year these tracks could lead to only one place, the winter den of the bear. I forgot about the elk I had been stalking and followed the bear.

The tracks led to the neatest den I ever saw or heard about. In a rather open stand of trees was an inconspicuous crevice in a limestone outcrop. The tracks led down and into an opening under the rocks. No tracks led out again, so here was my bear going into hibernation. . . .

From time to time I visited the place during the winter. The opening was completely covered with snow to a depth of three feet for almost four months.

Early in April Rush discovered the bear had come out of hibernation. Shortly afterward, Rush entered the den through the narrow crevice and found he could stand up in it. With his flashlight illuminating the den, he estimated it to be eight feet square. From ground level a slab of rock eighteen inches high and about five feet wide extended out from the back wall. The slab was littered with dead leaves, pine needles, and twigs, and evidence told that the bear had slept upon it, warm and safe from the wintery blasts of the high mountains, once the snow had drifted to close the entrance.

Grizzlies often have beds or nests along trails of their own making, and which they like to follow. At these places they lie up to rest when not feeding. Along their trails I have found they tear the bark from trees, as if one were blazing a trail. Their beds are well spaced along the trail and often are concealed by rocks or deep brush or ferns. The bed, or nest, is a hollow in the ground about five feet across by one or two feet deep, dug out by the bear. I have found them near creeks, lakes, natural salt and mineral licks, and from low valleys to high above timberline. All were littered with either leaves, twigs, pine needles, dead grass, weeds, or a mixture of some, or all. Most of them were on a hillside or slope, giving the grizzly a good view of his downhill back trail. At the same time, the bed was in such a position the bear could get the scent of an enemy from other directions by the air currents coming down from the higher elevations by way of draws, canyons, ravines, clefts, and so on.

On one occasion, while I was guiding a Chicago lawyer, we watched an old grizzly feed for an hour or more just out of accurate reach of our rifles. After feeding, it lumbered nonchalantly to the edge of a cliff overlooking a wide valley. It sat down on its haunches like a dog, and swung its head slowly and sedately from side to side as it tested the wind. After a time it moved up a seemingly unscalable slope to a bed where it took its midday nap. Since several hours would have been required to reach the bear, we left it snoozing peacefully.

Life and Death

A grizzly usually remains in the territory of his birth during his life span of from ten to thirty years. The average area of his home range is between twenty-five and thirty miles, or roughly twelve and a half to fifteen miles each way from a central point. Seldom do they travel farther. I have watched old grizzlies make the rounds of their domain, passing at a certain locality on their range about once every thirty to fifty days. There are exceptions, such as in the case of Old Club Foot, a nomadic stock killer. Many years ago he became so troublesome he was finally brought down after being trailed by Ben V. Lilly, a famous southwest predatory animal hunter, who followed him from New Mexico into Chihuahua and Sonora, Old Mexico, and then north into Arizona. Occasionally a grizzly will migrate and establish a new range, if hounded too consistently by hunters, if his food supply gives out, or if the bear population becomes overcrowded.

I have never seen or found a grizzly bear that had died a natural death. In Idaho's Sawtooth Mountains, early one spring, I came upon a grizzly that had been killed while feeding at the base of a slide. He was crushed between two huge boulders. Either another avalanche plunged down from the top of the slide, killing him before he could escape, or in digging under one of the boulders he loosened it and it toppled over, crushing him between it and the other boulder.

Personally, I believe the grizzly bears pass away in hidden caves or remote spots, or during their winter sleep. Russell Annabel, Alaskan guide, prospector, trapper, and big game hunter, states: "We have found the remains of two old grizzlies that died in their dens, which ended so far as we are concerned the myth that nobody ever saw the body of a grizzly that had died a natural death."

Very few animal-caused wildlife tragedies are ever come upon by humans. The reason is the injured animal invariably seeks shelter in some secluded spot where it remains until it dies; its body then is quickly consumed and scattered by predators and rodents.

Food and Feeding

The grizzly bears are omnivorous. Being both herbivorous and carnivorous, they are fitted by nature and instinct to feed upon both vegetation and meat. This wide range is entirely the result of environment. With few exceptions their feeding habits in any given region are identical.

Grizzlies eat sparingly the first week or ten days after coming out of hibernation. They begin by feeding on shoots of grass, skunk cabbage, and similar foods. Later they dig for roots, and in time increase their diet to a variety of foodstuff.

Their chief foods are roots, bulbs, grasses, berries, fish, insects, carrion, fresh flesh in the form of gophers, marmots, and mice. They occasionally kill deer, elk, mountain sheep and goats, but it is seldom a deliberate hunt on their part for meat. Such animals usually fall prey to grizzlies upon sudden meetings at close quarters, where the victim is often in a position from which it has little or no chance to escape, for a grizzly can charge with terrific speed in short distances.

In by-gone days grizzlies sometimes stalked the drag of a buffalo herd to obtain food. By following a herd, often a grizzly could bring down some aged, sick, or crippled animal, a straggler, or one that had been wounded by Indian or buffalo hunters.

In their journals, Lewis and Clark stated that the bears were particularly numerous in the vicinity of the Great Falls of the Missouri, where well-worn buffalo trails led down through the cut banks to the river's edge. Great herds wound down the narrow trails to drink daily. The press of oncoming buffalo often forced the leaders out into the current. Many were swept over the falls. The dead drifted ashore, providing a banquet for the grizzly bears gathered there. In this instance, as was the general rule, the grizzly did not kill, but fed upon animals killed under other circumstances.

The grizzlies of Idaho country are known to be vegetation and fish eaters, although they will kill and eat ground squirrels and other small rodents. They may spend hours digging them out. Except on very rare occasions, they have not been known to kill stock, or touch rotten or freshly killed animals.

In certain parts of the country, where elk and deer are still plentiful, grizzlies do depend on game to some extent for their food supply. But the game usually has first been killed by hunters or met death in some other fashion, such as being frozen. In early spring when feed is short, or in cases where it is still covered by snow, as a matter of self-preservation a grizzly will of necessity attack game. However, I am convinced grizzlies as a rule do not make a habit of hunting wild game.

Several times, in various parts of western Canada and our western states, I have seen grizzlies feeding close to deer, elk, mountain sheep, mountain goats, and domestic livestock, with the bears showing no tendency to molest them.

In springtime, and where mountains are very steep, melting snow sometimes causes great avalanches that sweep everything before them. When grizzlies first come out of hibernation they go to feed at these slides. The avalanches expose great quantities of grass, roots, and bulbs that were beyond reach under deep snow. New, tender shoots of various types of vegetation grow quickly when exposed to the sun by the slide, providing palatable delicacies for the grizzlies. There too, they find marmots, squirrels, mice, gophers, and other small animals that have been killed by the avalanche.

Unlike our common black and brown bears, a grizzly, due to his bulk and build, cannot climb a tree. He simply is not built that way. But when it comes to digging, he is a champion. I have watched them go over a stony area, overturning tons of small boulders in their quest for ants, grubs, gophers, marmots, and field mice. I have seen them move yards of dirt and rocks, taking an hour or more of time to dig out a ground squirrel from its den. Sometimes the intended victim escaped. If the bear succeeded, one gulping mouthful was the reward for his strenuous labor. Yet he would be satisfied, and soon start ferreting out another of the small animals.

Grizzlies are constantly on the prowl for food. I have watched

32

a grizzly knock off the top of an ant hill, bury his nose in the interior, and with a few inward breaths, like a suction pump, draw every vestige of life from the hill. When berries become ripe, the great bears will invade the wild berry patches. I have seen as many as four bears in one blackberry patch, all feeding peacefully as they broke, bent, and twisted brambles to get at the fruit.

When his fishing season starts, the grizzly knows it. He never gets mixed up on his dates. A few days before the first salmon run begins in his locality, he leaves the high country and works down the mountain side to the lower streams to be on hand when the fish appear. Grizzlies have their "pet" fishing grounds, which are usually at some shallow riffle, near concealing cover in which they can lie up when not fishing. In such a locality they will remain until the fish run is over.

The grizzly's most common way of fishing is to invade a riffle, pin down a fish with a paw, then take it in its mouth. Sometimes it will grab the fish in its mouth right from a riffle, or from shallow water where the fish has no chance to escape. The grizzly's two most prominent methods of fishing are by pinning the salmon to the bed of the stream with a forepaw, then carrying it onto the bank in its mouth, and, secondly, by scooping or batting the fish out onto the bank with a forepaw.

On the whole, the grizzly spends about seventy-five percent of his waking hours in search of food. Because of this, with a normal food supply, they are very fat in the fall. When they den up for the winter, this surplus fat carries them healthily through their long sleep until spring.

Fighting Ability

Stockmen, old-time bear hunters, a park ranger, a Forest Service man, and a Northwest Royal Canadian Mounted Police officer, all have told me they personally saw grizzlies fight, or knew other men of reliability who had seen and described them. I, personally, have never seen two grizzlies fight.

From the stories I have heard, when a grizzly does battle with another, he does not stand up on his hind legs, as he is often described and pictured as doing. He fights on all fours, sometimes rearing up to a half-standing position as he bites and tears with his powerful jaws, or smashes and slashes with his mighty paws and claws. No holds are barred, but throat grips and the crippling of the opponent's legs, neck, and back, along the shoulders, seem to be the predominating tactics used. Their fights are savage and terrific affairs, and some last a long time.

The Mountie told me of coming upon a huge, aged grizzly in northeastern British Columbia. It had been killed by another bear whose tracks revealed it to be a smaller and probably a younger animal. The deceased was clawed and bitten from the middle of his back to the tip of his nose. Hunks of fur and flesh had been torn from his body. One foreleg was broken above an almost severed paw. The dead bear's deeply gashed shoulders and neck were covered with blood-matted fur.

Clyde Luxe, cowman, guide, and packer of Idaho's Sawtooth mountain country, took me to a grizzly feudal ground he had come upon but three days before. From the looks of the place there had been quite a scrap. The fight area roughly covered forty feet square. Bushes had been beaten to earth, the ground had been torn up, and several pools of blood and chunks of hide and hair were scattered about. A third bear's tracks were present.

I have seen several grizzly battle grounds. Each of the fights took place in June, July, or August, the grizzlies' mating season. With the exception of two of the feuds, there were tracks of a third bear about the embattled area which, no doubt, was a female and the cause of the fight.

Until recent years I have always believed the grizzly to be king of the wild animals of the North American continent. In general, this may be true. However, several authentic accounts have come to my attention that show exceptions to this conclusion. Many years ago, my father found a young grizzly in Utah's Wasatch Mountains. It had been gored to death by a bull elk. It was the night after the first snowfall, and prints told of a short, quick battle between the two upon their meeting. My father followed the elk's blood-marked trail for half a day, but never saw him.

All in all, the grizzly wins most of his battles, for he is a fighter, and once riled he will attack man or beast with no consideration for the consequences to himself.

After much study and observation, I am convinced that the only animal feared by the grizzly is the timber wolf, which may weigh up to 120 pounds. Reliable wolf and grizzly hunters of Alaska and Canada say that the grizzly retains his fear of wolves until he is seven or eight years old. A full account giving in detail the actions of wolves against grizzlies is retold here in the words of Russell Annabel:

At the headwaters of Montana Creek one June, while hunting dens with a wolfer known as "Lobo" Smith, I witnessed an incident that, for my money, established the wolf as the undisputed tyrant of the Territory's [Alaska's] wildlife.

We had located a den under a red sandstone ledge at timberline, and were watching it with binoculars to find out how many adult wolves were there, when we saw a straw-colored female grizzly and two fat brown yearlings climbing toward the spot from the creek-bottom willows. As it turned out, the wolves had cached a quantity of meat near the den, and the smell of it decaying in the sun was what had attracted the bear.

Mountain wolves prefer to feed their pups rabbits, squirrels, and marmots, but sometimes a scarcity of small game makes it necessary to feed them the flesh of larger animals, which they transport to the dens in their bellies and disgorge for the pups. In this case, the ground outside the den was littered with gobs of partly digested and fly-blown caribou meat. I suppose the mess smelled like banquet material to the grizzlies, for in early June, when there is little green vegetation and the salmon have not yet ascended the streams, high-country bears are always hungry.

The grizzlies were fifty yards from the sandstone ledge when a large brindle wolf and a pair of cream-colored two-year-olds suddenly appeared in the rocks near the den. After watching the bears a moment, the brindle wolf raised his head and uttered a short howl. It must have been an alarm signal, because at once the bitch wolf shot out of the den. She was black as sin, a lean, ugly beast, long-legged and long-muzzled, with pendulous teats. Her mane rose so stiffly erect as she stared down at the grizzlies that it made her look humpbacked.

The she-grizzly had reared to try the wind when she heard the brindle wolf howl, but now she dropped back to all fours and continued up the hill, rolling her shoulders in an arrogant pigeon-toed swagger. If the wolves worried her, she didn't show it. But the two fat yearlings weren't so unconcerned. They stayed close to the she-bear's flanks as if expecting trouble. They had sense.

"Bet five bucks on the wolves," Lobo said.

I took the bet, feeling like a patron of the Roman circus. I was a sucker. In his time, Lobo had killed around 1,000 wolves. To do that you have to know a lot about the animal. You have to be good. Lobo knew his business all right, and he knew how this affair was going to end.

I was aware that wolves will fight with matchless courage when other animals come near their dens, but I didn't think they could shove grizzlies around. I had always thought that the grizzly was the dictator of the mountain game ranges, that he wandered where he pleased and fed where he wished to, no matter what animal's preserve he happened to trespass on. That was where Lobo had the advantage of me. He had seen grizzlies and wolves in altercations before.

The black bitch started the fight. She flashed down the slope, feinted at the she-bear, and went past to chop at a yearling's flank. An adult wolf of her race has fangs more than two inches long and jaws capable of cracking a caribou's leg bone, and in consequence the shearing cut she gave the yearling caused him to lose all interest in the fray. Squalling, he tried to crowd against his mother for protection.

But the she-bear had troubles of her own. As the three other wolves closed in, she spun like a top, roaring hoarsely, and launched terrible paw strokes that never quite landed. The wolves were too fast for her, they came in from too many angles at once, and she was handicapped by the yearlings. She edged toward a pile of rocks. Like a bear beset by hounds, she wanted cover for her back. She didn't get it.

The bitch wolf slashed again at the wounded yearling, and this time the luckless little bear fled blindly down the hill, bawling in pain and terror. Without hesitation the other yearling followed at great speed. The she-bear batted again at the elusive wolves, and then, roaring defiantly, lumbered after her offspring, which concluded the episode.

In a second story, Annabel tells of watching a female grizzly protecting her two cubs against five attacking tundra wolves. This was convincing proof that in some areas (Alaska) the grizzly population is stabilized by wolves killing cubs and even yearlings.

In a third account, Annabel gives the story of a grizzly's attempt to kill a cow moose's June calf—only to be put to shameless flight by the cow's slashing hoofs.

On the other hand, I found a bull moose killed by a grizzly. Tracks revealed how the bull, upon being surprised by the bear, turned and ran down a slope into a deep snow drift and became trapped, thus meeting his death.

Various accounts which have come to my notice, especially from the Alaska-Canadian areas, tell of the dog and bitch wolf trailing a grizzly mother, and sneaking up and hamstringing her cub. When the grizzly charged, the wolves simply sidestepped her and waited. Eventually she would go on, leaving her injured cub behind.

Ferocity

The fierceness of the grizzly is a subject upon which two hunters seldom agree, due to the fact that few hunters really understand the animal. The grizzly, with few exceptions, is a very curious, intelligent, courageous, and dignified animal, and not the ferocious and dangerous one he is often portrayed to be. His curiosity drives him to do impulsive things which frequently have involved him in trouble. The results cause him to be falsely accused of many things of which he is guiltless, or had no intention of doing. At heart, as close observations of his actions have shown, he desires only to be left alone.

If a grizzly hears a sudden noise, or sees a movement out of the ordinary, or something new or strange to him, his curiosity will immediately be excited and he will more often than not investigate, if he isn't afraid of it. Often he will stand up on his hind legs for a better view. If he fails to see clearly, his curiosity will be aroused all the more. Finally curiosity will get the better of him. Dropping to all fours, he will advance toward the point in question to investigate. About that time a nervous hunter will shoot. He tells how he was the victim of an unprovoked charge by a ferocious grizzly. The thing he fails to realize is that the bear, in almost every case, was merely trying to satisfy his insatiable curiosity and was handicapped by his poor eyesight. The grizzly's poor eyesight, no doubt, has caused him to be blamed for countless charges. Novice hunters do not realize the bear investigates to satisfy his curiosity due to his inability to see distinctly what it was that disturbed him.

Since most hunters hunt up-wind, the grizzly often receives no warning of their presence by scent. The grizzly has a keen sense of smell, far better than his eyesight. It is a known fact that when a grizzly scents a new odor, he immediately associates it with danger. Until he investigates the cause of the odor and satisfies himself about it, he will not dis-associate it from danger.

It is also a known fact that the grizzly, because of his immense curiosity, has a habit of following up any trail that puzzles or interests him, be it one made by man or animal. This trait erroneously seems to be an attack to the hunter who believes the grizzly to be a savage brute.

The grizzly is wary and alert, ready to give one the go-by if possible, and able to tax the hunter's ingenuity in matching his cunning. He becomes more cautious as greater caution is required, but even in the remotest parts of his range, he is no more on the lookout for a fight than any other wild animal. The fact that now and then an ugly, pugnacious grizzly is encountered is an exception, not the rule. This is not to assert that the grizzly will not fight. When it becomes necessary, or when he thinks it is necessary, there is no animal of his size that can put up a fight equal to his. When he does fight, he fights for keeps and gives no quarter. Nothing but instant death will stop one of his maddened charges. When brought to bay by dogs, it is extremely dangerous to go near him. He will then charge everything that moves, even every bush that shakes. A she-grizzly with cubs is at all times an uncertain customer.

In the Kootenai country of Montana, in 1914, Jim Lake, a trapper friend of mine, came upon a grizzly busily digging for rodents on a hillside. The bear was up-wind and about forty yards away when Jim stepped on a dry stick which broke with a sharp crack. At the noise, the bear quickly turned around, stood up, and looked down the slope. Jim, wearing a red and yellow lumberjack shirt, was partly concealed behind some bushes in brilliant fall foliage. With his shirt and the foliage blending nicely, he remained motionless, watching the bear swing its head from side to side in an attempt to scent him. Finally the bear's eyes settled in his general direction. A full minute passed before the grizzly dropped to all fours. In a lumbering walk it came straight toward Jim. When about halfway, a sudden shift of the wind must have brought Jim's scent to the bear. The bear stopped suddenly. Jim moved. The bear took one good, brief look at him, issued a throaty "woof," and moved toward some nearby timber. At the timber's edge it hesitated, looked back, and then, in a dignified manner, disappeared into the woods.

An unknowing man might have considered the bear's actions the start of a charge.

A study of the reports of famous western explorers, from the time of Lewis and Clark to present-day hunters, shows that charging grizzly bears, except in isolated cases, were first angered, surprised at close quarters, harrassed, or shot at by the party attacked. In many of the latter cases, the bear first tried to escape. This entry of May 6, 1805, from the Lewis and Clark journals, proves that even in their time all grizzlies when shot did not charge: "Captain Clark and one of the hunters met the largest brown bear [grizzly] we have seen. As they fired it did not attempt to attack, but fled with the most tremendous roar."

I have found that many grizzlies, if shot when they were not aware of the hunter's presence, will, for some undetermined reason, invariably run in the direction from which the wound is received. This is another reason why so many hunters claim that grizzlies have charged them. The first time this came to my attention, I had shot across a gulch at a grizzly prowling for food at the base of a slide. At the report of the gun, the bear charged toward me. He came up my side of the gulch, the brush swaying and cracking as he came tearing through it. When he came out of the brush he was about fifteen yards to my left. I was in a small clearing and raised my 30-06 to shoot again. He saw me, paused, turned quickly away, made about two jumps, staggered, and dropped dead.

Since that time, I had another grizzly do the same thing. On both occasions I was completely hidden from view, with the wind blowing from them to me. Both bears charged at an unseen enemy, in the direction from which the injury had come.

During my work with professional guides, I have seen several grizzlies run toward the direction from which their injury came. Because of this trait, I am certain they do not always do so with the intention of charging. Other hunters, and many old-time bear men whom I have met, confirm this action and are of the same opinion. On the other hand, if a hunter comes upon a grizzly at close quarters, perhaps surprising it, cornering it, or making it think it is cornered, the bear will usually charge and keep coming until his dying breath. I know of several cases where grizzlies have either wounded or killed men. In only one instance did I find where a grizzly turned out of his way, seemingly unprovoked, to attack a human being.

I have met several grizzlies under various circumstances. I have hunted him in remote regions where he had seldom been disturbed and have seen him change his habits as his range was encroached upon by man and his very existence threatened by the extinction of forests and the extensions of ranch and farmlands. But I have never found him the ferocious, ill-tempered, ill-mannered animal that he has been accused of being. The grizzly, as a rule, never seeks trouble and avoids it whenever possible.

On one occasion in New Mexico, I circled a hill. Upon recrossing my trail, I discovered tracks of a grizzly that I knew had not been there before. Upon following the bear's tracks, I learned he was following mine just a few yards to one side of my trail. As I rounded a point, I made considerable noise for safety's sake. I did not want any possible, sudden meeting to seem like an attack to him. Upon rounding the point, I saw him across a shallow draw. He was looking back along his trail, his head cocked in a position of curiosity, undoubtedly wondering what was the cause of so much racket. About the time I saw him, he saw me and bolted for a bramble patch, disappearing before you could say "scat."

The wounded grizzly is a fighter and especially so if encountered at close quarters and cornered, or thinks itself to be. When a grizzly is shot, the hurt naturally causes rage, which invariably brings on a direct charge; this I repeat again, if the bear is at close quarters.

Stamina

Weapons against the Grizzly

The early day smoothbore gun was a poor weapon against the grizzly. This convinces me that much of the talk about the grizzly being able to withstand terrible punishment has been inaccurately handed down through the years. I have found that they cannot stand any more punishment than deer or elk. W. H. Wright, a renowned, old-time big-game hunter, claims they cannot withstand as much shock or lead as a mountain goat, and in his time he killed more than one hundred grizzlies.

Long shots used at any kind of game may not hit true because of the distance and are inhumane since the game may escape to suffer miserably before death. This holds true many times, even with the use of telescopic sights. I favor a 30-06, but have used a 30-30 Winchester on one occasion, at close range, and found it most effective. I have killed five grizzlies; one with one shot from a 30-06, one with two shots; one with three shots from a 30-30, and two others with two shots each.

From the journals of Lewis and Clark, dated June 12, 1805, an entry tells of their coming out to the Missouri River from an expedition inland. On this day they saw two large brown bears [grizzlies] and killed them both at the first fire, "a circumstance which has never before occurred since we have seen the animals."

On other occasions, the journals reveal that members of the expedition fired numerous balls into bears, none in a vital spot, before they were slain.

James Willard Schultz, who wrote several books and many magazine stories about the Blackfeet Indians and their country in Montana and Canada, and who lived with them for many years, tells in several of his books of the Blackfeet killing grizzlies with a single shot from smoothbore guns. The Blackfeet at that time were using muzzle-loading guns obtained in trade

42

with the Fur Companies. Of one incident he writes: "She was broadside to me; this was my chance. I aimed close back of her shoulder, and well below the back, and fired . . . she was coming about as fast as ever, but suddenly, as she jumped, she died: died in the air."

The theory that a grizzly cannot be killed with a single shot is groundless. If the bear is hit in the head or heart, it will not run far because the impact of the bullet, especially of the mushroom variety, produces tremendous shock in spots that are vital organs. I have records where nine and eleven bullets were placed in the big bears before they were killed, but these were from smoothbore guns, a Kentucky and a Hawkins rifle, shooting 30 balls to the pound.

Warning! Never follow a wounded grizzly into intense cover. To do so is inviting suicide. Almost any wounded animal will attack one who is foolish enough to follow it into thick brush or fallen timber. A wounded grizzly is no exception, especially if encountered at close quarters, or cornered, or thinks itself to be. Renowned bear hunters agree with me that a wounded grizzly never charges while standing on its hind legs. All that I have witnessed came at the hunter on all fours, sometimes with a clamping of the jaws, or with a bawl or snort, but never with an open mouth.

The grizzly is just as easily killed with the modern rifle as any other wild game. The chief concern of the hunter should be to keep cool and put the bullet in the right place. If the hunter places the bullet in the center of the shoulder, or just back of it, or at the base of the ear, he will kill in every instance, and usually with one shot. Old bear men and most present-day experienced hunters unanimously agree on this point.

Blaming the Killer

Recorded stories are told by both Indian and white men of watching a grizzly follow a buffalo herd and eventually seeing it pull down an aged, or maimed, animal in the drag of the herd. This was a known practice of wolves. Due to these wolf-killings, grizzlies were blamed to an exaggerated extent for killing trail-herd cattle in the same way. It is now commonly known that most of such killings were done by wolves, but the grizzly was blamed.

Unless in the late stages of disintegration, it is usually easy to distinguish whether an animal was killed by a bear, lion, wolf, coyote, or bobcat. The professional hunters, trappers, and most stockmen know the different animal killer's marks, and from them know upon which to fix the blame.

The average grizzly, when he does consume meat, likes it in the rotting stage. When he scented such a feast, he followed his smeller to it. In the process of gorging himself, he usually destroyed the real killer's tracks. Consequently, in many cases in the early days, where a grizzly's tracks were found about a carcass, whether it killed the victim or not, the bear was blamed for the deed. Although a few stockmen knew differently and defended the grizzly, the majority at that period did not.

Close examination of a slain animal would have disclosed the modus operandi of the killer, for each predator has its own method of stalking and killing its prey. If such had been done, it would have cleared many a grizzly, even though his tracks had obliterated most, if not all, of those made by the real killer, or killers. Stockmen just didn't look for other signs. If tracks of the real killer were seen, the majority of stockmen in those days insisted that they were made after the grizzly had killed and left. Their attitude was, "A grizzly did it! That's all there is to it!"

Forest Ranger Wm. M. Rush, a man of wide experience with bear happenings in and around the Yellowstone Park area, voiced a similar opinion on this attitude when he wrote: "Tales of bears

44

killing stock are legion. There is no doubt that bear do kill colts, cattle, and sheep, but I believe the damage done has been greatly exaggerated by stock owners and their employees. If a bear happens to come along and eat from a cow critter that has died from poisonous larkspur, the owner of the cow will invariably blame the bear for killing his animal. And sheepherders are as careless with their accusations."

The grizzlies did not strike at their victims like a cat, as they have often been described as doing. They cuffed, clubbed, mauled, bit, clawed, ripped, and smashed. When they cuffed domestic sheep and other small animals, they usually crushed the victim's skull or sides, sometimes ripping them open with their claws in the process. Often they killed by hooking their claws into the neck, belly, or ribs, while knocking a "woolie" out of their way. Sometimes they tossed it into the air while doing so.

On large game, they killed by tearing their prey's throat with claws or teeth, or by biting or breaking the neck, or caving in the skull or ribs with club-like blows of their powerful paws. At the same time, they inflicted deep gashes upon the victim's body with their claws—or they just clawed and bit until their prey bled to death.

When a grizzly did kill, besides his tracks he left plenty of other positive evidence that he alone was the killer, regardless of marks and tracks made by other carnivorous animals who moved in afterwards.

I have only the records of two reliable eye-witness accounts of a grizzly killing cattle. One was told to me by Lon Duncan, and is related later. The other was told to William H. Wright, who used it in his book *The Grizzly Bear*. He writes: "It stole up close to a nearly fullgrown heifer and then, in a sudden spring, threw one fore paw across her neck, placed the other on her muzzle, and drawing up one hind leg with a single backward shove of its great claws, not only disemboweled her, but tore out all her ribs on that side."

Wolves, coyotes, and big, husky bobcats, especially in winter, and in the spring when cows are with newborn calves, cause heavy losses to range stock. They either hamstring their victims, large or small, tear the throat, or disembowel them with slashing fangs.

When deep snow is on the ground, the padded, pliable feet and lighter weight of wolves, bobcats, and coyotes allow them to race over crusted snow in fast pursuit of heavier, hard-hoofed animals which break through, become trapped, and consequently fall easy prey to the predators. Wolves and coyotes also hunt the snowdrifts for animals which have become trapped during storms. Many a horse, cow, moose, deer, elk, antelope, mountain sheep, mountain goat, and, in by-gone days, buffalo lost its life due to being caught in such a predicament.

Mountain lions, when attacking small domestic and wild animals, sometimes deer and mountain sheep, usually do so by stalking as near as possible, then rushing to climb upon the victim's back or shoulders. Then, with their powerful jaws, they break the neck, or tear open the throat. When they attack large animals, such as elk, horses, and cattle (they use this method also on deer and mountain sheep), they stalk their prey, or if possible, leap down upon the quarry from some high point, which is often beside a game trail or watering spot.

John D. Larrick, a Utah cattleman, witnessed a mountain lion's attack on a range mare in the Wasatch Mountain country. The following excerpt from his letter to me telling of it gives a typical, and accurate, account of a mountain lion's method of attacking large animals.

In mid summer of 1947, I was lying atop a rocky point watching a band of twelve brood mares grazing in a timberline valley, when I noticed a mountain lion. The cat was moving down a boulder and tree dotted ledge toward a water hole, which sat in a rocky pocket about one hundred yards below me.

He was a big fellow and the way he worked along, it was evident that he was hungry and on the prowl. Whenever he came to an open spot, he stopped and looked out on the meadow. Nevertheless, I'm convinced he didn't see the mares until he came to a draw some distance ahead of him, since it was at that point he froze in a half-crouching position. From then on he used all available cover to screen himself from them. Even though a breeze was blowing from the band to him, he still halted occasionally to eye them.

From his actions I felt confident that he had hunted in the vicinity before and he anticipated that the mares would eventually go to the water hole because he unwaveringly kept on going down the ledge toward it.

When the lion neared a big, flat top boulder beside the water hole, he dropped on his belly and crept slowly forward until he gained its top. There, he inched under the limbs of a scrub cedar canopying its top, until he reached the far side which was about twelve feet above the water hole's edge. There he shifted his body into a leaping position and lay still. Only the tip of his tail flicked slightly as he tensely eyed the band as it gradually fed toward him.

About then, realizing what I might witness, I became so engrossed in the anticipated wildlife drama that might transpire before me, the thought to kill the lion never came to my mind.

It wasn't long until the mares stopped grazing and came toward the lion. When the lead mare was almost to the water hole, she stopped abruptly, as did the others behind her. For a moment she paused, head held high, eyes forward, nostrils distended as she tested the air. Since the off-wind gave her no warning of danger near by, she became satisfied that all was well, issued a slight nicker and the band advanced, never knowing a sinister pair of eyes watched them.

Every muscle in the big cat's body became taught, ready for instant action, when the mares started forward. Five yards from the water hole the lead mare again stopped and tested the air. Again satisfied that all was well, she moved to the water's edge, as the other mares spread out on either side of her to drink. The last mare moved directly in front of the boulder upon which the lion crouched. She was less than fifteen feet from the lion. The moment she lowered her head to drink, the cat leaped at her with lightning speed. If he made any noise, I didn't hear it. At sight of him, panic gripped the band. For a split second they froze. Then they bolted for the meadow, but that split second's hesitation was what the lion must have depended upon, since the mare below him was too late.

As she threw up her head and turned to run, the lion landed solidly on her shoulders and embedded his fore-claws firmly into her neck. Seemingly at the same time his jaws closed on her neck just back of the head. Her terrified cry was cut short as the lion, with a mighty side swing, threw his hind quarters up and forward to catch her under her lower jaw with his hind feet, driving her head up and back to break her neck, where it joined the head. A second after the mare toppled to the ground, the big cat ripped open her belly and began devouring the liver.

About then I came out of the state of lethargy I had been in. My first thought was to kill the killer, but with my 30-30 in the scabbard on my horse, which I had left to graze behind the point, I was powerless to act. Consequently I immediately crawled from the point hoping to be unseen, but when I returned with the rifle, the lion had either seen or scented me, and was gone.

Mountain lions kill an average of fifty deer a year. They also take a heavy toll of cattle on summer range in the high mountain meadows. In his heyday, the grizzly all too often was blamed for these. A lion invariably covers a kill, intending to return to it, and often returns each night until the meat is consumed or becomes tainted. Lions will not eat tainted meat, but will make a fresh kill, whereas a grizzly will eat tainted and even rotten meat, but in no way does the grizzly compare with the common black, brown, and cinnamon bears who are the scavengers of the forests. A grizzly rarely covers a kill. I have seen but few of their caches.

In our present time, stockmen, and predator hunters in the employ of our state and federal governments, are well versed in the predator's killing habits, and seldom fail in placing the blame on the right animal.

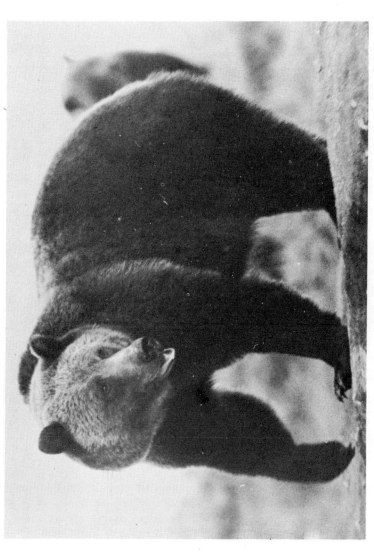

The finest photo of a mature, Wyoming grizzly I have ever seen. *Photo courtesy of David de L. Condon.*

Exceptionally light colored, young grizzly. This bear's pelage is much lighter on the body than is characteristic of the grizzlies of the Wyoming country. The picture was taken near Yellowstone National Park. *Photo courtesy of National Park Service.*

Beside the hide of Old Mose on the left, Henry Beecher, old timer, rancher and hunter of the Canon City, Colo., country. On the right, J. W. Anthony, who killed the notorious outlaw. The picture was taken by Warton Pigg in Wright & Morgan's Market in Canon City a few days after the grizzly was brought down by Anthony. *Photo courtesy of Janet Sterling.*

The Piegan Blackfeet Chief, Wades-In-The-Water, wearing the jacket and badge of the Piegan Indian Police, of which he was a member. Photo taken in 1923, at Washington, D.C., by D. L. Gill, B.A.E. *Courtesy of Bureau of American Ethnology, Smithsonian Institution.*

Exceptionally fine picture of a young grizzly's head. Note light, buff colored fur on top of face, head, and neck, and darker fur on upper part of lower neck. This color marking is typical of grizzlies of the Wyoming Rockies, and is the reason why they are often referred to as "bald-faced" grizzlies. Picture taken at Trout Creek, Yellowstone National Park, August 8, 1956. *Photo courtesy of David de L. Condon.*

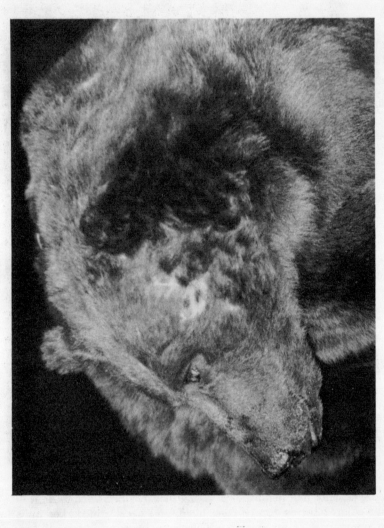

Night picture of an aged grizzly. Note battle scars in front and below left ear. *Photo courtesy of David de L. Condon.*

Resting grizzly cub, about six weeks old. *Photo courtesy of National Park Service, Yellowstone National Park.*

Sow grizzly and her two cubs. The color markings of all three bears were the same—rare in grizzlies. *Photo courtesy of National Park Service, Yellowstone National Park.*

The Longhorn vs. the Grizzly

When the ever westward movement of pioneers eventually exterminated the buffalo and brought the longhorns in their stead, a new era of livelihood was opened to the grizzly. This era began about 1867, when the first herds of longhorn cattle were being trailed north from Texas to be shipped east from the railheads in Kansas, or to stock the ranges of Wyoming and Montana. It was at this time that occasional articles of grizzlies harassing trail herds began to appear in the newspapers of the period. Several eye-witness accounts of battles between grizzlies and wild, or half wild, belligerent longhorn bulls, and even cows, were recorded, especially in Wyoming, Colorado, and western Texas. (Cattle were trailed from Texas to Montana as late as 1895.)

The sight and scent of a grizzly will usually cause wild game to race away, but domestic cattle and sheep, as a rule, do not. Horses, particularly wild ones, will run or keep at a safe distance, but a number of recorded cases tell of wild stallions and mares with newborn colts who have turned to give battle with grizzlies.

Like the buffalo, longhorn cattle, especially with calves on the open range, formed a compact circle around their young. This also applies to horn bearing cattle of today which have been raised on what remains of our open range. In such a position, with hindquarters to each other, they presented a defense of sharp horns with which to fight the attacking grizzly, or other predators. Although many a bear, wolf, and coyote met his death in such an engagement, they, nevertheless, took toll of stock in such encounters.

Carl Schroder, cattleman, and in later years a professional guide and packer, told me of seeing such an action in the spring of 1893 in the foothills of Beaverhead Mountains in Montana.

During the morning of a late May day, a snow squall covered the ground with about two inches of white. During the squall some horses had broken out of a corral at the line camp where

Carl was working. When the skies cleared in the afternoon, he rode to the bluff-like point of a timbered ridge. A break in the trees allowed him to scan the surrounding country. He halted his horse and searched for any sign of the missing animals.

Unable to locate the horses, Carl watched five cross-bred Durham-Longhorn cows and their calves come up a wide draw that cut through a ground swell between the point and the ridge across from him. Near the middle of a small hollow, about two hundred feet below, was a big spring, shadowed by the ridges. All the cows had good sets of horns. Carl saw the cattle drink at the spring and move out on the hollow and begin to feed on clumps of grass. One by one, the cows lay down in a circle and their calves lay down within the circle.

All were soon peacefully dozing. Suddenly a two-year-old, medium brown grizzly came over the ground swell by the draw. He stopped short when he saw the cows and calves. The wind must have been blowing from the wrong direction for either the bear or the cattle to scent each other, but a sudden cross current of air evidently carried the bear's scent to one of the cows. She awoke with a snort and sudden spring that brought her to her feet. Whirling about, she lowered her head and faced the grizzly. Instantly the other cows sprang to their feet and with lowered heads also faced the bear. As all snorted loudly, the hair on their necks bristled up like that on a mad dog's back. Quickly shuffling about, they formed a circle with their hindquarters to each other, their sharp-horned heads facing outward. The calves had gotten up on their feet with their mothers. In fright, two of them started to run away from the others. They made only a few leaps when a commanding snort from one of the cows brought them scampering back to dart under their mother's bellies and disappear in the center of the small circle formed by the cows.

The grizzly had frozen at sight of the cattle. Presently he relaxed a little and shifted a forepaw uneasily as he continued watching the small herd. Shortly, at a slow walk, the bear started to circle them at a safe distance. In hope of finding a sleeping calf, he made a zigzag course from one clump of nearby brush to another. He continued to keep his distance as he circled the menacing horned heads, knowing that to come too close might result in a goring or cutting hoofed death.

He completely circled the herd, stopped, stood up on his hind feet and issued several threatening "woofs." He advanced a few feet and repeated the woofing. The cows snorted defiance and pawed the ground threateningly, but never gave an inch. After several more bluffing attempts to stampede the herd, the grizzly dropped to all fours and lumbered away to disappear beyond the ground swell. He knew if he could not stampede the cows and pull down a calf in the confusion, their numbers were too many for him successfully to attack alone. Range cows, especially with calves, are too wise to break a circle under such circumstances.

Carl had no firearms with him, but if the grizzly had attacked the cows a boulder rolled off the point would probably have scared the bear away.

The highly bred, corral raised, hornless, and thus practically defenseless cattle appeared in the last years of the grizzly's glory. When attacked, these cattle usually just stood still, too frightened to know what to do, and were pulled down without a fight. Sheep normally bunch and stand helpless when a grizzly, or other predator, walks into the flock, wantonly killing right and left the defenseless "woolies."

Mountain lions, wolves, coyotes, and bobcats, as a matter of record, kill more livestock each year in our present time than all the outlaw grizzlies put together ever did. In many cases an act of their doing was laid to an innocent grizzly, solely because the grizzly came upon the carcass and, in gorging himself, destroyed most of the real killer's tracks and left his own.

The grizzlies had their greatest success with the rugged, lone-critter longhorn, or with a single cow and calf. Many gave battle, often strewing fur, hide, and gore over a trampled battleground. A fair percentage of these conflicts ended with a proud, if bloody and weak, longhorn stalking away from a much mangled, gored, and sometimes dead, grizzly.

While checking the history of a Colorado outlaw grizzly known as Buff, the story of a death-battle between the bear and an outlaw longhorn bull named Blaze was discovered. Buff was the only outlaw grizzly I could find that was killed by another animal.

Buff was so-named by stockmen because of his brownish-tinged, buff-colored pelage. He was credited with slaying many elk and deer, several horses, over one hundred sheep, and eighty cattle. Some of the latter were imported animals of good blood, and accounted for the high reward of $750 on his head at the time of his death in 1894. His history was interesting, but research brought out too much conflicting testimony to be able to compile a reasonably accurate account of his entire career. The death fight between Buff and Blaze was seen and described to me by Lon Duncan, a professional hunter.

Some cattlemen in the San Juan Mountain country hired Duncan to hunt Buff down. Whenever Buff reached a certain district on his range, he spent several days in the vicinity of a mineral spring. This spring sat at the back of a pocket located near the head of a blind canyon. The pocket had a narrow entrance, and was lined with sheer, rocky walls about sixty feet high.

The next time the grizzly headed in the direction of the spring, Duncan took a short cut, figuring to get there first. Before daybreak he hid among boulders atop one of the walls near the entrance to the pocket. The pocket was small, flat, and open except for some brush near the wall across from him and part of an aged, fallen tree near the spring. When daylight came he saw Buff's tracks at the spring. The grizzly had been there during the night. The wind being right, Duncan decided to wait, knowing from past actions that Buff usually visited the spring a couple of times before he left the area.

After a while he heard something coming. Soon, a big, blaze-faced, roan-colored bull, with white hindquarters and legs, came through the entrance and advanced halfway across the pocket. Duncan recognized him right off as the crossed Hereford-Longhorn bull cowmen about the country called Blaze. Blaze was about twelve years old. Since branded when a calf, he had never been held in a roundup. During roundup he hid out in remote spots. He was battle scarred from fights with other bulls, and old, deep, claw-marks on his neck and shoulders showed that he had tangled with a mountain lion or bear at one time. Looks told he held up to his reputation of being wild, cagey, and tough.

After standing still for some time, he advanced to the spring. He paused, sniffed Buffs' tracks, then raised his head and tested the wind. Just as he was about to drink, he whirled around with a loud snort, made two long jumps, stopped abruptly and threw his head up. The hair on the back of his neck stood straight up and his tail kinked in a high arch. His muscles stood out all over him. He looked a power of strength and defiance.

Duncan followed the longhorn's gaze, and there, almost directly below him was Buff, standing up on his hind legs. Duncan had not heard him approach. The bear was holding his forepaws up a little in front of him, his tongue lolled out. His head was bent slightly forward. The intent expression on his face was one of mixed satisfaction and known advantage. He seemed to sense, in his position before the pocket entrance, that he stood between the bull and escape.

Blaze began snorting, pawing the ground with his forefeet, and flinging his head in a defiant manner. Buff suddenly dropped to all fours and began a cautious advance toward the bull. As he moved forward, Blaze backed up until his hind feet were in the spring. Then he moved forward and sideways, all the while keeping his sharp-horned head low and toward the bear. When they were a few feet apart, Blaze bolted forward. At the same time, Buff lunged into a half-standing position almost in front of the bull and struck forcibly with both forepaws. His left paw caught Blaze below the neck and cut deep gashes on his chest. The other paw landed solidly behind his shoulder. The two blows knocked the bull down. He landed in the brush amid a mighty crash. In falling, he instinctively twisted his hindquarters and kicked with both hind legs. His sharp hoofs cut deep slashes on the grizzly's chest. The bear went over backwards with a bawl of rage and pain. For a big animal, Blaze moved quickly. He was on his feet before Buff was. When the grizzly turned to face him, he lunged forward and drove one horn into the fleshy part of Buff's shoulder. With a powerful flip of his head, he tore the horn free just as the bear bit a chunk out of his shoulder. They separated and began circling each other.

61

After several threatening starts on the part of each of them, the bull followed through. Buff half rose as he turned sideways to avoid the charge, but one horn caught him just under the left front leg, going clear through the leg muscle and coming out along the shoulder. Buff bawled with rage, hooked his claws into Blaze's side and back, and tried to bite the top of the bull's neck just back of the head. If he had succeeded, he would have probably broken the bull's neck. The constant moving of Blaze, along with the horn against his shoulder, prevented this. Consequently, he vented his fury by clawing and biting Blaze's shoulder and side as best he could. They were stuck in that position for a good quarter-minute. All the time the bull was forced by the bear's weight and movements to hold his head down and sideways. Nevertheless, using his front legs as a pivot, he kept moving his hindquarters away from the bear, keeping the grizzly from attempting to climb on his back. Buff followed up the movement, not only in an attempt to get at the bull's body, but also because of the horn hooked in his shoulder. Finally Blaze gave a mighty uplift with his head and moved sideways, drawing the horn free. Then he struck savagely at Buff with a sharp hoof, missed, and backed away.

Both of them were covered with blood. The left side of Blaze's neck and shoulder was a mass of torn flesh where the bear had raked and pounded him with claws and paws. Blood ran from gashes and horn punctures on Buffs' chest, sides, and shoulders.

They weren't apart long. The grizzly made a wild head on charge. Blaze met it with a lunge and upswing of his head, just as Buff started to rear up on his hind feet. One horn tore a long gash on Buff's chest, and went on and up into the bear's mouth from the underside of the lower jaw. This drove the grizzly's head back and held it in a useless position. Blaze kept driving forward. As the bear was pushed backward he blindly smashed and clawed at the bull's head and face. They were a few feet from the fallen tree when Blaze gave a bellow and with a mighty heave threw the bear clear and backward. The grizzly came down against the log with a bawl of pain. A sharp crack of breaking wood sounded simultaneously. In his backward fall, the bear had come down on one of several short, jaggedly pointed limbs along the top side of the log. It went in behind his rib area and came out back of the left shoulder. The force of the fall snapped the limb off the log. Both ends of the limb were sticking out of Buff's body. Blood was spurting from wounds on the bear. Blaze's nose was almost torn away; his face was a mass of shreaded flesh. He kept flipping his head in what seemed to be an attempt to get the blood out of his eyes, all the while bellowing low from pain and anguish.

After lying beside the log for several moments, Buff got up. He was clamping his teeth in sullen rage as he wobblingly started for Blaze. Blaze saw him coming and hooked a horn into the upper part of his right hind leg. It went clear through and twisted and held Blaze's head downward. Buff hooked one paw under the bull's neck; with his other paw he dug the claws into the shoulder. In that position the grizzly stood on the leg hooked by the horn and, with his other hind leg, reached up and forward in an attempt to hook his claws in front of the bull's ribs by the shoulder. If he had succeeded, he would have tried to tear the ribs out with a tremendous backward thrust. Buff had weakened from loss of blood and was slow in his actions. Blaze pivoted on his front legs and circled away from him. The bear missed his hold for the ribs, and Blaze broke free. As they parted, Buff's claws under the bull's neck tore the throat badly. Blaze struck twice with a hoof at the bear, ripping a gash in its belly. Buff issued a pained woof and staggered blindly about. Parts of his intestines were dragging the ground. Suddenly he dropped to the ground. Once he tried to rise, but his life's blood was about gone. He sank back, his head slumped forward. He was dead.

Blaze was standing spraddle-legged, his head down, and was trembling all over. Finally he stumbled over to the grizzly. Amid a mixture of groaning snorts, he jabbed at him with a horn. Blaze, bleeding badly, was about done for. Hesitantly, he moved through the pocket entrance and disappeared from view.

Duncan grabbed his rifle and ran down a draw to the canyon. Near the pocket entrance he came upon Blaze beside a huge rock. He, too, was dead.

Duncan skinned both animals and had their heads mounted

just as they were. Blaze was clawed from the end of his nose to the middle of his back. Several chunks of hide and flesh were gone from the fleshy parts on the sides of his neck. His throat had been torn half open. One eye was gone. His horns measured three feet ten inches across. They were thick at the base, with a good curve out and upward near the rather sharp pointed ends. His weight was estimated at 1500 pounds. A check on the bull's breeding revealed he was five-eighths Longhorn and three-eighths Hereford.

Buff weighed 887 pounds. He had twenty-seven gashes on his body that were inflicted by the bull. The grizzly was between fifteen and eighteen years old. Several of his claws on each forepaw had recently been broken off. If they had been full length, he would have done much more damage. The limb from the dead tree measured three feet one inch in length. Duncan kept it over his fireplace for years. When entering the bear, the limb had cracked two ribs, besides tearing a vein leading to the heart.

The battle area was about fifty feet square. All of it was sprayed with blood.

Another illustration of the longhorn's fighting qualities was told by my father. While in Juarez, Mexico, in 1883, he witnessed a pit-fight between a big longhorn bull and a full grown grizzly. After being savagely bitten and clawed about the neck and head, the bull threw the bear completely over his shoulder, turned quickly, and gored the bear to death.

Although a domestic animal, the longhorn was always courageous enough to stand and face the grizzly singly on any field of battle. This was undoubtedly due to the longhorn being endowed with the spirit of self-preservation, plus the knowledge and fighting blood gained through generation after generation of battle for existence against drought, flood, blizzard, and carnivorous enemies.

As civilization continued to move westward and large stock ranches came into being, the grizzly in various areas was pushed back to the remotest parts of his once vast domain. However, as a whole, the great bears soon made it clear that they would not move out altogether just because man had decided to move in.

The grizzly quickly learned that, although longhorn cattle held their ground and put up a terrific battle, most cattle were easier to approach than the buffalo and other wild game occasionally attacked in the past. This was especially true in the early 1890's when the chunky, meek, hornless, pasture breeds of cattle, such as the Hereford, began displacing the belligerent longhorns on the range.

Since the coming of man into their domain caused much of their natural food supply to be cut off or restricted to certain areas, the arrival of livestock gave the grizzlies a very good reason to stay where they were and they began to kill an occasional cow, sheep, or horse. In rare instances a few of these bears developed an elusive cunning and continued to kill stock for food. Therein lies the beginning of the livestock-killing grizzly. Only a minority of them, in a short space of time, became outlaws in the eyes of stockmen and a price was put upon their heads.

Man vs. Grizzly Encounters

In justice to the grizzly, it must be said that his awesome reputation comes in large measure from his size. His bulk has naturally bred in him less fear than in smaller animals. However, a few years after he met white men his boldness became hesitant caution, except when cornered or attacked. If a charge could be avoided, he would try to escape.

In early time the silver-tip, known to the Indians in general as white-bear and to the Blackfeet Indians as real-bear, ranged down upon the great plains. Journals of the Lewis and Clark expedition state that the men found their forward progress rendered hazardous at times because of grizzlies. J. Fields, a member of the expedition, was pursued by three grizzlies in eastern Montana, and escaped only by leaping over a steep cliff at the risk of his life. Near the great fall of the Missouri in Montana, Lewis was chased by a grizzly. To escape, he plunged into the river up to his waist and presented the point of his espontoon (a sharp spear-like weapon then used in the army) to the bear. The grizzly tested the water, found it too cold for him, and retreated.

Hugh Glass

As mentioned, the grizzly showed little regard for the smooth-bore guns of the early explorers and trappers. The case of Hugh Glass shows this quite well.

Glass was in a group under Major Andrew Henry's direction in the 1820's. Major Henry led the group on a trapping expedition into unexplored Montana country. Near the present Wyoming-Montana line, Glass jumped a she-grizzly with two cubs. Glass shot the she-bear with his smoothbore gun at close quarters. The bullet had little effect on her. She charged and was upon him before he could reload and fire again. Glass drew his knife and stabbed her time after time while she was mauling him. The grizzly suddenly dropped dead.

When other members of the party found Glass, he was still alive but unconscious. He had been frightfully injured. His entrails were exposed about the stomach area and on his back. Since the expedition was in hostile Indian country and in no position to carry an injured man—also believing that Glass could not live—Major Henry offered a reward to anyone who would stay with Glass until he died. A man named Fitzgerald volunteered.

Exactly what happened afterward will never be known: either Fitzgerald thought Glass dead, or he became panicstricken at being by himself in hostile country. He left Glass. Glass regained consciousness and crawled and rolled his way to water. He lived for some time on berries growing near the water. As he gained strength, he decided to try to reach Fort Kiowa, a hundred miles away in the Dakota territory.

His back injuries prevented him from walking. He started the long trek to the fort by crawling on his hands and knees. Water aided his feverish body greatly; it also helped him keep the injuries to his stomach clean. Blowflies laid eggs in the wounds on his back and the worms that hatched from them ate away the poisonous flesh, preventing infection. For food he lived on berries, frogs, and other small creatures that he could catch.

He came upon a buffalo that had been killed by wolves and gained strength from the meat diet. When ready to crawl on, he tied some of the meat to him for future use. When the buffalo meat had been consumed, he came upon an abandoned Indian camp. Several dogs had remained at the camp and Glass managed to kill one of them with a sharp instrument he found there. The dog meat provided more food for his trek. One type of good providence followed another and in time Glass reached Fort Kiowa, completing the greatest march for survival the West has ever known.

Upon complete recovery, Glass returned to the Montana country, vowing to find Fitzgerald and cut off his ears. History records that Glass never caught up with the man.

Few men have killed a grizzly with a knife and survived.

In 1890, William Parenteau, mine foreman for the Gunnell Mine near Central City, Colorado, rode into the rough Boulder Park country one morning to hunt for deer. At the mouth of a gulch he tied his horse and continued on foot. A snow had fallen the night before. Finding deer tracks, he followed them. In a short time he came upon the tracks of a big grizzly and her cub. The bear tracks crossed those of the deer. Parenteau left the deer tracks and began trailing those of the bears. At an open spot he stopped short. A large grizzly was across the gulch from him. The bear was swinging her head from side to side, trying to locate Parenteau's position by scent. The bear was too far away to shoot. The gulch was brushy and full of down timber, so to keep the bear up-wind until he could get closer to her, he made a half circular movement. When he gained a position from which he could see where the bear had been, she was gone. Parenteau went back to the place from which he had first seen the bear.

When a noise sounded behind him in the brush, Parenteau knew what had happened. While he had made a half circle to get nearer the bears, the bears had made a half-circle to get at him. The she-bear, thinking he was after her cub, meant to destroy him.

Before Parenteau had turned completely around, the grizzly came crashing out of the brush. Just as he fired, the cub cut between him and its mother, exciting him and thus deflecting his aim. The bullet did hit the she-bear near the shoulder, but it only increased her wrath. The bear was then so close Parenteau had no time to reload and fire, so he used his gun as a club. The bear knocked it from his hands. Drawing his long bladed hunting knife with the intention of striking repeatedly at a place low down behind her shoulder, where he thought the heart would be, he faced the then half-standing grizzly. With a lunge she knocked him down and grabbed an arm in her mouth. When she relaxed her hold for a moment, he tore his arm free, only to have her grab his head in her mouth. When she closed her powerful jaws he almost fainted from pain. While she held, chewed, and twisted

68

his head in her mouth, Parenteau almost passed out, but during it all he had presence of mind enough to keep driving his knife into her side. When the grizzly suddenly fell over, everything turned black before Parenteau.

Regaining consciousness, he realized the grizzly was lying beside him, dead. Parenteau was nearly insane with pain. His right eye was nearly gouged out. The bear's tusks had punctured holes in his neck. The right side of his face and his nose had been mashed and torn by the powerful jaws. His scalp hung in front of his face. One leg was badly injured and his right arm and shoulder were mangled and unusable. He managed to get to his feet, search for and find his rifle and reload it. He feared the cub might attack him due to the smell of blood. Then he began hobbling his way back to his horse. He could not recall how long it took him to reach the animal.

The horse reared and plunged at the sight and smell of Parenteau, but he finally got the saddle on its back and mounted. He started the horse for a sawmill about three miles away. That was the last thing he remembered for days.

Late that afternoon, beside a mill building, an employee named Williams came upon the horse with the slumped form of Parenteau still in the saddle. How long the horse had been standing there no one knew.

Dr. T. L. Ashbaugh was sent for. Upon his arrival he had Parenteau immediately taken to a hospital in Denver. More than one hundred and fifty stitches were taken on his head and face. In a year he had fully recovered and returned to work, whole in body, but self-conscious of his disfigurement. The right side of his face was badly twisted and scarred.

Allen Hasseldorf

Another survivor of a hand-to-claw encounter with a bear was Allen Hasseldorf. Now over seventy years of age, he lives on his homestead at Mole Harbor on the Admiralty Island, Alaska. His encounter was with a huge Alaska Brown, the largest animal Hasseldorf had ever seen.

Hasseldorf shot at the bear on a beaver meadow, and it went down. Believing it to be dead, he turned his back on it to place his rifle against a bush and to draw his bowie knife. Turning around, he saw a mountain of fur directly before him. The bear's left forearm and paw was limp and drenched in blood from the wound in its shoulder. Hasseldorf was too near the bear to reach his rifle before the enraged animal could grab him.

Being an experienced bear hunter, he admitted he should have waited longer before laying his rifle aside. However, he did the next best thing. He dived into a shallow beaver ditch, face down. The bear mauled him, taking a bite out of his shoulder. Hasseldorf felt his flesh being torn away, then fainted. When he regained consciousness the bear was gone. After much pain and hardship he reached help and medical attention. Hasseldorf's courage and knowledge of lying still when attacked by a bear saved his life.

The Strongest Medicine

The San Felipe Pueblo Indians of New Mexico still tell the story of four of their men who fought four grizzlies near the turn of the century.

The men, two of whom were armed with rifles and two with bow and arrow, had been hunting deer in the Jemez Mountains. Late in the afternoon they started down Peralta Canyon toward their village. They were traveling along a ledge when suddenly they came face to face with a she-grizzly and her three cubs, which were about eighteen months old. The Pueblos had a healthy respect for the grizzly, as is true of all Indian tribes, but the meeting was so unexpected and close that the four men had no chance to escape up the narrow ledge before the she-grizzly attacked the man nearest her. In the ensuing fight, the grizzlies killed three of the hunters and severely wounded the fourth.

The she-grizzly was killed by gunfire, as was one of the cubs. The cub rolled off the ledge while thrashing about in its death agony. The other two were slain by arrows, driven feather-deep into the bears at a distance of only a few feet.

The surviving hunter staggered into the village late at night. He lived, but one arm and shoulder, torn and smashed in the encounter, remained useless the rest of his life. As the crippled hunter once put it in telling of the encounter, "Our medicine was the strongest."

"Bear" Moore

Few people today have ever heard of James A. Moore. For years he was referred to as "Bear" Moore. At the time of his death in 1924, New Mexico newspapers gave him heavy publicity because of his early history and misfortune.

Disaster overtook him in 1883, near the headwaters of the Gila River in New Mexico. He and his partner had a temporary hunting camp there. Both men were professional hunters, supplying soldiers at Fort Bayard with mule deer meat.

One morning they left camp, Moore going one way and his partner the other. Moore encountered a huge, mahogany-chocolate colored grizzly. He and the bear were on opposite sides of a big log. Moore could see only the top of the bear's back above the log. He shot at the bear and thought he hit it in the spine. Believing the bear had dropped and was dead, Moore started around the log. The wounded bear was moving down the log toward the same end Moore was approaching. As they rounded the end of the log, the bear attacked.

Moore's partner found him that night. His heart was exposed and beating. The grizzly was dead nearby. The bear's intestines were strung out over the ground and a skinning knife lay between Moore and the bear.

Moore was taken to Hermosa, New Mexico, and given emergency treatment, then moved to St. Louis, Missouri, for additional surgery. He lived, but half his face was gone and his neck was horribly scarred.

Moore returned to New Mexico and stayed at the Charles Rathburn Ranch for awhile. People began calling him "Bear" Moore. Conscious of his condition, he allowed his hair and beard to grow long in an attempt to cover his disfigurement. Later he

71

moved into the hills and lived as a recluse for years, trapping and panning a little gold in Turkey Creek.

Recent Encounter

At the time of this writing, the most recent death of a man caused by a grizzly is reported from Augusta, Montana, in 1956. The report follows:

HUNTER KILLED BY BEAR

Augusta, Montana, October 22, 1956 (AP) A Fort Benton, Montana elk hunter was fatally mauled in a western Montana wilderness area by a wounded grizzly bear. The victim was identified by his brother, Donald, as Kenneth Scott, 29, Loma area farmer.

Another hunter, Vic Squires, Fort Benton, received a claw wound in the foot in the skirmish between the two hunters and the bear Squires described as "huge."

He said the incident occurred in the Bob Marshall Wilderness area about 40 miles west of this central Montana community Saturday afternoon.

Lived 9 hours

He said Scott died of injuries early Sunday about 9 hours after the fight.

Squires gave this account:

The bear "jumped" them as they were looking for elk. He backed up, tripped in the brush and the bear grabbed his ankle, sending a claw through a heavy logging boot. Squires kicked. The bear reared up and noticed Scott on a knoll.

Scott fired two .30-06 slugs into the bear which then retreated.

The hunters decided to track down and kill the wounded bear before it could kill or injure others in its enraged condition. After tracking for hours, they found the bear and Squires emptied his clip of .30-30 shells into the bear.

Gun Jammed

Before he could reload the weapon, the bear began to charge. Scott fired two .30-06 shots at the bear. His gun jammed and he yelled to Squires to run for safety. Squires thought Scott was running too.

Squires then went to camp to get the other six members of the hunting party.

They returned to find Scott severely injured and the bear gone.

72

They took Scott to a river bank for first aid. The bear again surprised them, but was felled by two slugs in the neck from a .30-06 rifle fired by Morrie Embleton, 23, Fort Benton.

The bear dropped dead about 10 feet from the party.

Intensive research about grizzlies has failed to uncover an authentic case of a grizzly eating human flesh or remaining for any length of time near a human that it had attacked. Evidence is convincing that the grizzly only attacks a human due to being startled at close quarters, in defense of its young, upon being cornered or when it thinks itself to be cornered, or because of a wound injury. Once enraged by man for any of these causes, however, the bear seems to lose control of his temper and senses. I say this because I believe another factor many hunters do not realize when they are faced with a charging grizzly is: subconsciously the hunter, under such circumstances, has a touch of fear in his system which creates a scent given off by his body. The grizzly detects this fear-scent which, along with his rage, increases his boldness and temper beyond the point of reason or caution. When the man object is rendered motionless, or remains so, the bear's fury abates and it gains control of its senses and soon retreats.

The grizzly definitely fears the human scent and dislikes the smell and taste of human blood. This opinion seems to be commonly agreed upon: records reveal it to be a proven fact time after time.

The following incidents from recent newspaper and magazine accounts, while not pertaining to grizzlies, are worth including to show the desperation of a wounded bear under different circumstances.

On September 4, 1956, the Denver, Colorado, *Rocky Mountain News* carried the following item:

Black Bear Mauls Denver Man After Breaking Free From Trap

Steamboat Springs, Colo., Sept. 3 (AP)—A 1000 pound black bear, trapped near a Northwest Colorado sheep camp broke free from the trap and mauled its intended executioner before it was killed Monday.

Leo Roybol, 48 . . . suffered severe fang and claw gashes on the head, arms, hands and hips.

Roybol and an unidentified companion, who killed the bear as it

73

mauled Roybol, rode three miles on horseback to a rancher's cabin at Clark, Colorado, about 20 miles north of here. The rancher, Lee Connor, then drove Roybol to Routt County Memorial Hospital, where he is reported in good condition.

Sheriff Ab Ritter said Roybol and his companion were employed at the sheep camp by the Cow Creek Sheep Co. of Baggs, Wyo., which had obtained permission to trap a bear which had been raiding the sheep herd.

Roybol and the unidentified man rode to the trap Monday morning, and saw the huge animal trapped by one paw.

The men dismounted and Roybol fired one shot at the bear.

The bullet struck the bear's head, and emerged at the back of the neck. Maddened, the animal ripped loose from the trap and charged Roybol before either of the men could fire a second shot.

The bear bowled over Roybol and shredded his arms, face, and body. Roybol's companion, waiting for a clear shot, finally shot the beast and killed it.

The two men then rode to Connor's cabin at nearby Clark.

Investigation verified this item, except that the bear weighed 400 pounds.

In writing of the Alaska Brown Bear, Cory Ford, well known writer and hunter, cites the case of a rogue Brownie. He states that the huge Alaska brown bear, often referred to as the Kodiak, is the largest carniverous animal on earth; that adults weigh around 1200 pounds, and in some cases much heavier.

"According to official census," Ford writes, "there are fewer than 5000 left in the world. Most of these are found on Admiralty and Baranof Islands in Southeastern Alaska, along the bleak Alaska Peninsula, and on Kodiak Island, whose whole interior has been set aside as a Federal game-management area with controlled hunting.

"Under normal conditions, a brown bear will not attack a man, provided the man doesn't challenge the bear's right-of-way in the trail. Unprovoked charges are rare. A bear can kill, but according to Charlie Madsen, dean of Alaskan guides, there has been only one authenticated fatality on Kodiak Island in over a quarter of a century.

"Often an injured bear will escape, to nurse a festering wound and a prejudice against the human race. One of these so called

74

rogue bears was responsible for a rare tragedy on the Kenai Peninsula a few years ago. King Turman, a trapper on Chickaloon Creek, was filling a bucket at a stream when he was jumped by a crazed brownie. The bear tore off his right arm at the shoulder and opened up his entire side. Half delirious, Turman crawled to his cabin, penciled a note with his left hand to explain what happened, and blew out his brains with his revolver. A posse was formed and the rogue bear was killed. Dissection revealed that the bear's jaw had been shattered sometime earlier by a bullet; the animal had gone mad with pain."

Grizzly Bears of Montana

TWO TOES
1902-1906

In 1902, Caleb Myres was working for a cow outfit in the Bitter
Root River Valley near Hamilton, Montana. In early spring a
stockman named Michaelson bought a mixed herd of cross-
bred Longhorn-Durham and Longhorn-Herefords from the outfit.
Michaelson wanted some of the hands to help drive the herd
north to his spread in the Swan River Valley, between the Flathead and Mission Ranges near Rumble Creek. Myres went along.

One night they camped near the rail town of Bonner. Lem
Cole, the trail boss, rode into town, got in a mix-up, and was shot.
Michaelson put Myres in charge of the eight other riders and the
cook. Myres started ramrodding the outfit north.

They were about ten miles southwest of Elbow Lake when
Myres first became acquainted with Two Toes. The outfit had
slowed down because a few cows had calved and were pretty
weak. Some of them were strung out behind the drag for quite
a distance. The men had rigged up a calf wagon for the little
fellows and it was full.

This particular night they put the calf wagon alongside the
creek, not far from the chuck wagon, and placed all the calves
on the ground, about twenty of them. The cook was to keep his
eye on them while working up the night bait. The wrangler took
the cavey out and the rest of the men went to the herd, which was
about a half a mile away.

At dusk the weak cows straggled in to the calf wagon, bellowing for their calves. Being busy at the dutch oven, the cook didn't
pay much attention to the cows and calves. Suddenly he heard
a quick movement among them and a brief, agonized bawl of a
calf. He ran to the front of the chuck wagon to get his 30-30,
which he kept behind the seat. As he moved toward the cows,

76

they scattered. He saw the bulky form of a grizzly beside a downed critter. He fired at it, but being excited he missed. Before he could shoot again, a critter got in the way and the bear escaped in the brush along the creek. It had killed a calf and a cow. On top of that, in the morning the men found they had two orphans with no cows to care for them.

After starting the herd north, Myres took a man and rode back on the trail about three miles. They found two dead cows, both killed by the bear. During the night a good part of them had been eaten by wolves and coyotes. A big grizzly's tracks, with half the right forepaw and two toes missing, was nearby. It was the same track that had been seen near the calf wagon. The next day they reached the home range and turned the herd loose. Myres was so busy with other things he forgot about the bear.

Along in the summer, Myres went to Missoula. There he met an old trapper and hunter named Ricks. Myres told him of the grizzly encounter, and about the two missing toes. Ricks took Myres to his room and showed him the two toes attached to a shriveled piece of bear paw.

Four years before, in 1898, Ricks had been trapping in the Mission Range below Elbow Lake. When the snow began to melt, he came upon some fresh grizzly tracks. Wanting the hide, he killed a buck near where he thought the bear was resting. After dragging the buck to a tangle of blow-downs, he cut it up and set two bear traps around it. Each was chained to a small section of a tree that had broken up in falling. Two days later, Ricks went back. The ground was all torn up. Deer entrails and bloody bear tracks were all about the place. The bear, one trap, and the section of tree it was attached to were gone. In his tussle with the trap, the bear had dragged the tree section out of the blow-downs and down a slope for a quarter of a mile.

Ricks found the trap with chain and tree section still attached. The bear had torn and chewed his paw free. Pieces of his teeth were on the ground where he had broken them off in biting the trap. Ricks said the tree section was too heavy for him to lift, so the grizzly's strength must have been tremendous. Ricks followed the trail for over a mile before he sighted the bear entering a stony ridge about three hundred yards away. Signs told the bear was male. Ricks judged him to be about ten years old and weighing close to 900 pounds. He was yellow-brown in color with long fur over his shoulders, a beautiful specimen. After Ricks showed the piece of paw and toes to the men about the country, the stockmen referred to the bear as Two Toes.

Ricks said that in 1900 Two Toes raided a chuck wagon belonging to the E-Bar-L outfit, while the boys were out on roundup. The cook was away at the time. When he returned, he found Two Toes had climbed into the wagon and raised merry-ned with his supplies.

During the same fall, Ricks said the bear charged several hobbled horses belonging to some Blackfeet who were hunting near Youngs Creek. He killed three horses before the hunters chased him off. They claimed to have wounded him.

Myres' story was the first report Ricks had heard of Two Toes attacking cattle. The bear had used the range southwest of Elbow Lake, and Rick thought it had probably trailed the herd northward. He had never heard of Two Toes being near the Swan River before, although there were still a lot of grizzlies west and northwest of the lake.

Ricks was right. Two Toes had established a new domain. Michaelson's Running M outfit was in the middle of it. In the fall he began giving them trouble. Soon after the first snow they found a few dead critters, all badly mauled. Knowing he was in the vicinity, several of the men went hunting for him, but never saw him. Possibly, he had hibernated. His toll of stock from the outfit stood at seventeen head.

During the winter, Michaelson became involved in a mining deal in Anaconda and lost most of his money. Myres did some fancy financing and bought the Running M from him.

When spring came, Two Toes returned to his happy hunting ground and the calves really caught it. In six weeks time Two Toes killed fifteen calves and three cows.

Myres got hold of a hunter and trapper named Kline. He tracked the bear all over hell-and-gone for three months before he spotted him stuffing himself on a range mare.

Kline was on a river bluff, too far away for accurate shooting. While he was sneaking up on him, the bear got his scent and watched Kline until he was almost to him. Then he skidaddled for some timber and brush beside the river. Kline fired. Two Toes staggered and nearly rolled over. Then he started for the timber again. Kline shot just as he reached it. The bear let out a bawl and disappeared in the thick underbrush. A bloody trail told he had been hard hit.

The patch of timber was small. Kline circled it twice. No bear tracks led out of the stand. Kline was an impatient fellow and made the mistake of following the bloody trail into the timber. Kline said later that he approached and followed the trail carefully, and always kept sight of the bear's prints well ahead of him. However, the bear made a fishhook turn in the timber and came back to squat close to his original trail of entry. Kline said when he came abreast of a briar tangle he heard a snarling growl and the crashing of brush. Instantly he knew what had happened. The next moment the grizzly was almost upon him. Kline fired once, maybe twice, grazing the top of the grizzly's rump. The bear smashed at Kline. Two Toes caught him just under the left arm pit, knocked him sailing and out cold. While Kline was unconscious, the bear chewed up and broke his left leg. When he came to, the grizzly was gone. Kline dragged himself to the river bank. That was the last he remembered until a prospector found him there the next day.

Back-tracking, the prospector found Kline's gun, a 45-70. The stock was broken and the heavy barrel was bent. They laid Kline on a mattress in a buckboard and took him to a hospital in Missoula. He lived, but leaned to his left and limped for the rest of his life.

Two Toes didn't bother the stock again until the next spring. However, that fall, as back-tracking afterward revealed, he spent two days following a JF trail herd on the way to the railway shipping pens at Bonner. A little south of the Flathead Range, he slipped into the herd and killed two steers. In so doing, he caused a stampede that cost the life of a horse and four steers that had to be shot because of injuries. During the next three years he attacked two other herds in the same manner and in about the same locality.

Because of a little rustler trouble about that time, several of the cowmen got together and formed an association. Along with a standing reward of $200 on rustlers, they put $200 on Two Toe's head. He had accounted for around forty head of stock, and they knew they hadn't seen the last of him.

With the spring of 1904, he began killing calves. He came down one side of Swan River for ten miles, then went back up the other. Twenty-nine calves were killed in that area, and several cows and steers. He would crush the calves' bodies with a smashing blow and leave them. One or two he had eaten; a few had a bite out of them, but most were just killed and left for coyotes and wolves. With older stock he would break their necks, tear out their ribs, and claw them from end to end. He killed several colts and a mare or two at this time.

In mid-summer he left Myres' range, crossed the Flatheads, and raided stock on the foothills of the old Seven-Up outfit's spread. Later he came back, crossing the north end of Myres' outfit and on into the foothills of the Mission Range. It was easy to find his kills and from them to check his movements. A cow would bawl, buzzards circle, or coyotes, wolves, or bobcats would race for cover when the men rode near them. Close by they would find a dead critter with tell-tale two-toed tracks about it.

In the fall, Myres made a night camp near the junction of a little creek and Swan River. Behind the camp a timbered hill ran parallel to the river. Beyond the hill was a valley where some cattle ranged.

The next morning he rode to the valley to have a look around. Through an open space near the crest of the hill he passed a bee tree, a hollow, rotten stump. When Myres came back, it had been knocked over and broken apart. Honey was all around it and Two Toes' tracks were everywhere. From bear signs and his horse's reactions, Myres judged the grizzly must have just left, probably scared off.

On one side of the clearing a long boulder and timber-covered ridge ran up to the crest of the hill. On the other was a low rise with a lot of open spots flanked with buck brush and trees. Myres tied his horse, took his 30-30, which wasn't a grizzly gun, and followed the bear's tracks. They led to the top of the hill and then crossed into the boulder ridge. When they led down the ridge, Myres reasoned the bear was on his way back to the honey. A second after he thought of his horse, he heard a terrified squeal followed by a short cry of pain. That was all. He hurried down the ridge, but too late. Two Toes had either heard him coming or scented him. Myres heard the bear crashing through the brush as he reached his horse. The horse was stone dead. The grizzly had caught him in the back of the head with a sweep of his paw, and had nearly torn his head from his body. Myres felt like a fool for tieing the horse. He was one of the best all-round cow horses Myres had ever owned. The saddle was clawed to pieces and ruined.

Not long afterwards, old man Ferguson, who had a small outfit to the north of Myres, and his two sons were hunting some missing horses near timberline in the Missions. They were keeping their eyes open for Two Toes, too, for he had killed a couple of their stock.

One afternoon about the time the sun was getting low, they came to a narrow pass that led across the mountains to the town of Polson. At a spring in the pass, they came upon the grizzly's two-toed tracks. The tracks were fresh and led over the pass. In that pass the east wall is about two hundred feet straight up and the west one about one hundred and fifty feet. Near its base it cuts back, making an overhang at the top. The Fergusons decided to quit looking for the horses for the time being and hunt for the grizzly.

They were about half way through the pass when they heard the pounding of horses' hooves on the hard ground along the rim above them. Thinking it might be their lost horses, they crowded under the overhang, so as not to be seen and scare or turn them.

Then they heard voices.

They were about to holler a welcome when one of the boys pointed to the opposite wall of the pass. There, about halfway up, they all saw the sharply defined shadows of ten men on horseback, riding over the crown of the rim above them. The first and last man carried rifles, the butts resting in their groins, the barrels pointing skyward. They were white men. The Fergusons knew that the eight men in between were Chinamen from their odd clothing and flat-top, wide brimmed hats, along with the awkward way they sat their horses. They reasoned the whites were smugglers because they knew a smuggler could get $1000 a Chinaman in Missoula, Anaconda, or Butte. They knew, too, smugglers ran them in from the Canadian line, traveling mostly by night, and they figured this bunch were being pursued by the law to be moving in such a hurry in broad daylight.

Realizing all that, and knowing men under such conditions are "bad medicine," the Fergusons, not wanting trouble, hugged the bank until they left. Remembering there had been local rustling trouble, they became more suspicious. They quit the grizzly's trail for that of the smugglers. The smugglers kept back in the foothills, turning south near the valley. When they were near Elbow Lake, a storm blew up and the trail was lost. The Fergusons stopped at Myres' place on their way back and told him of the incident.

Myres' men kept a close watch on the stock, but before long twenty head of steers were stolen. Like the Fergusons, they put two and two together and figured the smugglers were the ones who had been stealing cattle in the vicinity, bringing Chinamen south and taking steers north. The next spring the border patrol caught them.

Two Toes' toll of stock for that year was recorded at fifty-five head, and the reward was raised by $150. The cattlemen hoped to induce some professional hunter to spend the coming spring looking for him, but none did.

Two Toes was smart. He would never go near poisoned carcasses, and went around traps as if there had been a sign posted beside them.

All during 1905 he was never seen, yet he raided over three ranges and killed more than twenty-five head.

Once he killed two range bulls within a mile of Ferguson's ranch buildings. On that morning a cowhand saw ravens circling a creek bottom. Investigating, he found the dead bulls. They had been fighting. One was younger than the other. Both were of crossed Hereford-Durham blood and had good sets of horns. The younger bull had been killed first. Tracks showed that the grizzly had surprised and attacked him while he was battling the other. He had gone down at the bear's first rush, which had come from some brush bordering the creek. The other bull had then turned his fury upon the grizzly. They had fought a long time before the bull went down. Blood, fur, and pieces of hide were on the fighting grounds. Two Toes moved to another section of his domain soon after the bullfight. Ferguson hunted for him with dogs for some time, but never got on a hot trail. That fall the reward was upped another $100.

The winter of 1905-1906 was the worst Myres ever experienced in Montana. The snow came early and kept piling up. It was so bad they were feeding close to eight hundred head at each of their two line camps and about fifteen hundred at the main ranch.

The snow completely covered the food supply of elk, deer, and mountain sheep. Starvation drove them from the high country to the river valley. They were so hungry and weak that Myres had over two hundred of them feeding among his cattle at the ranch and camps. The corrals wouldn't hold the stock, so runners were put on the hay-wagons and hay scattered over the snow near the corrals. Hunger made the wild animals bolder and they followed the wagons, along with the cattle, to get at the scattered hay. The whole thing was a pathetic sight. The amount of hay had to be cut down and just enough feed used to pull them through. They were all pretty weak. Despite the feeding, about six hundred head were lost. Two-thirds of that number were caught in blizzards before they could be moved to the ranch or camps. They died from exposure or starvation.

Range conditions were terrible when spring did come. With so many other problems, nobody thought about Two Toes. When the bear came out of hibernation, a good foot of snow still covered the valley. As it melted, mounds appeared, scattered over the range, and under the mounds would be cattle that had starved or frozen to death during the winter. When a long chinook melted the snow, coyotes, wolves, and bobcats had a holiday. While looking for cattle, the riders shot the predators at every opportunity. More than seventy of their hides were nailed on the barn, or hung over the corral logs. Hundreds of deer and elk had died, too. Their gaunt carcasses were found almost everywhere there were cattle.

Despite all the dead animals dotting the range land, the men began finding recently killed cows with Two Toes' tell-tale marks about them. The critters didn't have strength to run or fight. The grizzly just walked up to them and knocked them over. Until well into the summer he kept traveling in a big circle that covered the ranges of several outfits. He must have destroyed twenty or thirty head during that time. Then he went into the high mountains and killed a few colts and one or two elk calves. He never came back to Myres' range, but made a few scattered kills that fall on neighboring ranches.

At the next association meeting, the grizzly question was taken up in earnest. The reward was raised another $125, and an experienced trapper and hunter, a French-Canadian named Belieu, was hired. He was guaranteed the $575 reward, plus $100, if he got Two Toes for them.

While waiting for the bear to come out in the spring, he trapped wolves and coyotes on the ranches of association members. When winter ended, he concentrated on Two Toes.

The bear led off by killing a cow elk. It was found in a wide draw leading up to the high mountains. Signs told how he had met a small band, rushed upon it, and killed the cow. Belieu had two airedales that took after the bear, while he followed on foot. When he came upon his dogs, one was torn almost in two and the other had its back broken. The loss of his dogs, which were his pride and joy, so enraged Belieu that he swore he'd stay on the bear's trail until he got him.

Not long after this, at a line camp on the Seven-Up ranch, six cowhands were branding colts. About sixty head were in the bunch, including the mares. They were turned out of the corral when the branding was finished. The horses started for a valley that lay beyond a narrow draw in a timbered hill behind the camp. Beyond the draw was a creek, heavily flanked with willows on the far side. When the horses reached the creek, they drank and then spread out to graze along its banks.

Four of the cowhands left camp as soon as the branding was done. The other two, Hawkey and Moore, were having a smoke in the shade of a corral when they were startled by the panicky cry of a colt. At first they thought a mountain lion had attacked the herd as it passed through the draw. They ran to the corral where they kept their saddle horses and heard another colt squeal just as they finished saddling. Close upon it came the agonized cry of a mare. They galloped for the creek. As they emerged from the draw, which abruptly ended near the creek, a big grizzly suddenly raised up at the edge of the willows.

At the sight of the bear, Hawkey's horse pitched and threw him to the ground. Moore's mount turned at the same time and banged into Hawkey's. Both horses fell with Moore on top of the pile. In the fall, Moore's head hit one of the saddle horns. Dazed, he got to his feet just as Hawkey's .45 roared twice. Moore found himself facing the grizzly, which was about fifty feet away across the creek. He drew his .45 and fired point blank at the bear. About then their horses went between the men and the bear. When the horses were out of the way, the grizzly was just disappearing into the willows.

Hawkey had broken his right arm in the fall, and had shot with his left hand. When his head cleared, Moore crossed the creek to the willows. There he found a dead colt and a dying mare. At the edge of the willows, he found another colt dead. It had been lying down when the grizzly came out of the willows beside it. Just then Hawkey's gun roared again. Moore came from the willows in time to see the bear cross the creek and disappear into the timber lining the upstream. A heavy trail of blood led into the brush and trees on the hill. All this happened within a few minutes.

Both men recognized Two Toes' tracks. They figured he was done for, the way he was bleeding. At the line camp, Moore set Hawkey's arm in a temporary splint. Then he took up the bear's trail. When night came he had covered close to four miles, all of it up a boulder and tree studded ridge leading into the Flatheads.

Later developments showed that only one bullet hit the bear on the inside edge of the left fore-leg, a little below the second joint. This was the last notorious event Two Toes pulled off.

Belieu kept after the bear all summer. He killed three grizzlies and several black and brown bear, but he never came near Two Toes. While the grizzly was destroying stock on one side of the Flatheads, Belieu would be on the other. When he would cross over, the bear would cross back to where Belieu had just left.

This was done three times that they knew of. All the old man did was keep him on the move. Several times tracks revealed how Two Toes would circle a hill or cut back on a ridge to get behind and watch the hunter who was hunting him.

In the fall two eastern sportsmen went into the Flatheads hunting elk and bighorns. A guide and packer named Thomas, from Missoula, supplied the outfit for them. He had a man named Dale helping him and doing the cooking. They spent several days in the mountain meadows until the hunters got elk. Then Thomas decided to move camp to an abandoned cabin and corral at timberline, where they would be nearer the bighorns on the high peaks and ledges above.

The morning they broke camp, Thomas and the hunters rode for a ridge where they had seen bighorns. Dale, with seven pack horses, started for the timberline cabin by way of a canyon. The two parties were to meet at the cabin that night. The fall air was crisp and the first snowstorm of the season was expected anytime, but on this particular day, the sun was shining and by midday it was comparatively warm.

Dale neared the head of the canyon around noon. At that point, the trail was at the foot of an open slope of loose rock with a low pinnacle bluff at the top of the slope. The other side of the canyon was lower, with a scattered stand of trees upon it. At the bottom of the canyon, a good quarter mile below, a turbulent stream thundered down the mountain. A few yards ahead of Dale the trail narrowed to make a sharp turn with the treacherous drop off to the creek on one side, and the sloping bank of loose rock on the other. This bank was studded with giant boulders that had sheared off the pinnacle bluff above. All in all, it was a bad spot to have trouble.

The pack horses were ahead of Dale. Two were out of his sight around the turn when one of the other horses let go a whistling snort of alarm, which brought the rest to an abrupt stop. A rock rolled onto the trail from the bank above. Then several more. As Dale looked up the bank, a yellowish-brown grizzly raised himself on his hind legs and looked down at him. The bear was about twenty-five yards away. In rising, the grizzly had started more rocks rolling. One bounced and hit a pack animal. The horse squealed and bolted in panic. The front horse in the remaining line bucked, but made it around the turn. The others, in a frenzy, reared up and tried to turn about on the narrow trail. One went off and fell to his death in the canyon. The other three took several steps up the bank, trying to turn. Then the grizzly let go a woof and a growl, and charged them.

Dale's horse became uncontrollable as it lunged up the bank in turning. By that time all four horses were jammed together. The pack animals were on an angle a little above Dale and between him and the bear. As he drew his '86 model 45-90 from the scabbard, the grizzly slipped on the loose rocks and rolled over with a startled bawl. As the bear quickly righted himself, Dale, from his frantically pitching horse, got the chance to shoot. The grizzly answered with a snarl of rage and pain and lunged at the animal nearest him. Amid the general confusion of sliding rock, the charging bear, and the terrified squealing and pitching of horses, Dale got in another shot. The bear's head and neck dropped. Then his body did a half-flip as it fell sideways and broadside to Dale. By that time the pack horses were out of the way. His own horse was a little above the trail and had crowded against a huge boulder. He fired the moment his horse stopped moving. The bear thrashed about as it tried to regain its feet, then relaxed and slid to a stop on the bank about twenty feet from Dale.

Dale's horse was moving so fast at the height of the action that he would see the bear one instant and the bottom of the canyon next. He said he had never come so near death as he did in that mix-up of grizzly, horses, and canyon drop-off. When he dismounted, he was trembling like a field of wheat in a windstorm and his horse was shaking from fright. The only thing he remembered right then was the dripping of the bear's life blood as it ran from its mouth onto a rock.

Dale's first shot hit the grizzly in the ribs, smashing into the lungs; the second broke his neck. The last one connected with the skull above the left ear.

The bear was Two Toes, all right. He had a lot of scars on his body. Three were old bullet wounds. Another, in the left foreleg was comparatively fresh. It was, in all probability, the one received in the recent encounter with Hawkey and Moore. The longest of his claws measured three and three-quarters inches along the top outside curve. He was sleek and fat.

Where Dale first saw him, a hollow in the rocks had been scooped out for a nest. Signs indicated it had been used many times. Undoubtedly, Two Toes had come up near timberline to hibernate, which he would have done soon after the first good snow. The day being fairly warm, he had gone to the nest for a snooze in the sunlight. The pack horses had awakened him and, in his somewhat cornered position, he had charged.

Myres saw Two Toes' hide after it had been made into an open-mouthed rug. The whitish hairs on his glossy coat marked him as more than 15 years old, possibly 20. He weighed all of 1100 pounds. His original teeth were in the open-mouthed head. Most of them were broken off. A few were missing, probably the result of his encounter with Rick's trap.

The cattlemen were glad to give Dale the $575 reward. Two Toes was a persistent killer. If he had slain only an occasional critter for food the cattlemen would not have cared so much. But he was a hunter who often deliberately stalked his prey and after destroying it frequently never ate a mouthful. He had killed an estimated $8,750 in livestock, all types included, belonging to association members.

Grizzly Bears of Montana

OTHER MONTANA GRIZZLIES

Montana, perhaps, had more bona fide stock-killing grizzlies of note than any other western state. Some of them raided for a couple of years, some only a few months. Old Montana papers and Stockmen's Association records mention their escapades time after time. The most prominent, other than Two Toes, were Peg Leg and Old Roughhouse.

Peg Leg, in his early life, lost his right forepaw in an encounter with a dead-fall trap. He was a cattle killer and ranged the foothills of the Rockies along the Teton River, a little northwest of Choteau, Montana. After a four-year killing spree, a Flathead Indian, Long Spear, killed him in 1911.

Old Roughhouse was primarily a sheep killer, although he destroyed cattle several times. He roamed in the foothills and vallies between the Tobacco Root and Madison Ranges east of Virginia City in southwestern Montana. He gained his name by the way he crippled sheep in the flocks he invaded. He was killed by a sheepherder in 1901, after harassing flocks for three years. Before migrating to the valley, he killed sheep in the mountains northwest of Dillon, in Beaverhead County, seventy miles from the Tobacco Root Range.

A grizzly's nose, like the nose of any species of bear, is the most sensitive part of his body. John Barnett, an old-time cowman friend of my father, sent me the following story, pertaining to an encounter he witnessed between a grizzly and a badger, wherein the badger dealt the bear untold agony.

In the fall of 1919, in the foothills of the Pryor Mountains east of Pryor, Montana, John tied his horse to a windfall, took his 30-30, and continued on foot, up-wind, to the point of a ridge. Upon rounding the point he saw a young grizzly about fifty yards away at the base of a slope. The bear had its back to him and was

89

digging. John thought the grizzly had a rabbit cornered in its hole. John wasn't bear hunting, but being interested, stood quietly to see the outcome.

The bear kept working away, throwing out rocks, dirt, and sod-clods. Once he stopped, blew his nostrils clean as he shook his head, then poked his nose into the tunnel-hole for a good sniff. He went back to work harder than ever. He was digging furiously when suddenly he jumped backward. He landed stiff-legged, and began pulling backwards, violently shaking his head and slapping at his face with a fore paw. With a choked bawling roar that sounded of pain, rage, and surprise, he raised up on his hind legs. With him came a full-grown badger, its powerful jaws locked over the top end of the bear's nose.

John saw immediately that the badger had an advantage. It had a powerful nose-hold and was sideways to the bear's mouth so the bear couldn't get it in its jaws. Too, the badger had twisted its body back, sideways, and down under the bear's jaws, all the while keeping its four long, strong clawed paws busy raking the grizzly's face, under jaw and neck.

The bear bent forward a little. Keeping up its bawling roar, it slapped and cuffed, crazy-like, at the badger, always just missing it. With that and the badger's claws all flying at the same time, John said he never saw so much action in so few seconds.

Blood began to spray from the bear as the badger kept ripping gashes in his face and neck. Suddenly the grizzly put a paw on each side of his head, about even with his ears, and swiped forward along his face with terrific force. The bear's right paw caught the badger broadside, tore the badger loose, hurling it into the air. The badger hit the ground ten feet up the slope, dead.

With blood spraying all directions from his face and nose, the grizzly dropped to all fours, fell over on his side, and as he bawled and thrashed in pain, he kept pawing at his nose. John decided to put the grizzly out of his troubles and get some bear meat at the same time. A slug back of the bear's ear did the trick.

He found the bear's face was a mass of cuts. One eye had been torn out, and the whole top-side and end of the nose was gone. The badger was torn almost in two, being held together only by

90

its backbone. Locked in between the badger's jaws was the bear's nose.

The badger is a treacherous and vicious fighter, but until I heard of this match, I would never have believed a badger would tackle a grizzly and hold on until death.

One of the most tragic wild animal predicaments I have ever heard about was seen by two hunters who had stopped to rest in a forested clearing northwest of Marysville, Montana. Suddenly they heard the sound of crashing brush and the pain-filled frightened bawling of a bear.

They climbed upon a boulder nearby and saw a six-months old brown bear cub blindly stumbling about as it bumped into rocks, logs, brush, and trees. Realizing something was amiss, they shot the cub. Upon examination, they discovered the cub had been totally blinded by porcupine quills. They found the spot where the cub had been lying beside a log for some time. Upon scenting them, and attempting to get away, the cub had attracted their attention and met a merciful death.

Grizzly Bears of Montana

AN INDIAN LEGEND OF REAL BEAR

The oldest story that I can find of a livestock-killing grizzly in the Northwest United States, although a legend handed down by word of mouth, tells of a bear which preyed on the horse herds belonging to the Piegan Tribe of the Blackfeet Indians many, many years ago.

The story of this bear came from Chief Wades-in-the-Water of the Piegan branch of the Blackfeet nation, during the summer of 1942 when he resided in Glacier National Park, Montana. He was 71 years of age, a fine, honorable, and wise man, true to his tribe and its traditions. He was a full-blooded Blackfeet, son of Running Crane, chief of the Lone Easters band of the Piegan Blackfeet. He was said to have been born in a tipi on the Marias River, Montana, and to have been named as an infant by an elderly woman. At the age of 14, he scalped an Assiniboin Indian. He participated in many native ceremonials, including the Sun Dance.

For many years Chief Wades-in-the-Water was chief of the Indian Police on the Blackfeet Reservation at Browning, Montana, and was one of the group of Piegans who were selected to greet and entertain visitors at Glacier National Park. He spoke little English, but was an accomplished sign talker. He died of pneumonia at the Blackfeet Indian hospital on the Blackfeet Reservation, Montana, on September 20, 1947. Much admired and respected by tribal members, his passing was a tragic day for the Piegan Blackfeet, since he preserved many historical legends of the tribe in his remarkable memory.

In 1860 the Blackfeet nation covered an area roughly defined as follows: It stretched eastward from the Rocky Mountains for a distance varying from 250 to 300 miles; it extended from the North Saskatchewan River in Canada southward to the north bank of the Yellowstone River in Montana. This vast territory was controlled by the three tribes comprising the Blackfeet Nation. The Siksika, or northern Blackfeet, roamed from the North Saskatchewan River southward some 250 miles; the Kainah, or Blood, or Central Blackfeet, controlled the country south from their northern brothers to about fifty miles below the present United States-Canadian line; the Pikuni, or Piegan, or southern Blackfeet, roamed southward from the Blood country to the northern bank of the Yellowstone River.

At our first meeting, Chief Wades-in-the-Water was reluctant to talk because his own people were fast taking up the white man's ways. The tribe was disintegrating and not preserving their tribal heritage or learning its history. He felt his people should hold to tribal ties and keep them and the legends and the tribe's history intact while adapting to white men's ways for the survival of the tribe. The younger members of the tribe were disinterested, while I, a stranger, sought the very information they were ignoring and discarding. Once he was assured that Blackfeet blood was in my veins (my mother was part Piegan Blackfeet), his reluctance left, and through an interpreter we had several days of most interesting conversation.

During one of our talks I asked if he had ever encountered a grizzly, or recalled the Blackfeet ever having trouble with an animal destroying their horses, for in the early days the Plains Indian's wealth was judged by the number of horses he might own.

"When I was ten summers (1881)," he said, "my father, Running Crane, who was thirty-four summers, showed me a grizzly bear-claw necklace. One claw was strangely twisted. The claws were from a brownish-grey furred grizzly of large size that had killed some of our horses and caused death to many others. When he was nine summers (1856), my father got the necklace from his father. My father's father told him this story of the bear":

The Account of Real Bear
as told to Chief Running Crane by his father.

When I was two summers [about 1820], the Piegans went north to

93

visit our brothers the Blood. Our brothers from the north, the Siksika, came south to the Blood camp, which was in the Red River valley. [Alberta Province, Canada.] When all the members of our three tribes were together, we numbered about 10,500 people. Such a meeting of our Nation happened seldom, and consequently there was much visiting, dancing, feasting, celebrating, giving of gifts, and sacrifices to the Sun. [The Blackfeet worship the Sun.] We were together but a short time. When the encampment broke up, we started southward as it was nearing time for the fall buffalo hunt.

We had traveled two suns southward toward our own homeland. At night our horse herds, some large, some small, were grazing around the camp and were watched over by herd boys and warriors. Our horses, owned by different warriors of the tribe, numbered about 2000. During this night there was a mass stampede of our entire horse herd.

At first it was thought an enemy had raided the herd and, since horses scare easily, especially at night, had started all the others into fearful flight. Our warriors mounted their best horses, which they kept picketed near their lodges at night, and rode out to give battle, but no enemy could be found.

When daybreak came, at the point where the first horses had started to run, the warriors found the remains of a colt and the body of a mare. Tracks revealed they had been killed by a big "Real Bear." At the bear's attack, the herd, in panic, had become uncontrollable by the herd boy and had dashed into another herd, and that herd into another, and on and on until all our grazing herds were in excited flight.

It took our warriors much time to recover the herds. Some horses were injured, some were found with broken legs, and some escaped.

We moved southward when the affair was over, driving the horses in several large groups—intending to separate each owner's animals later. We didn't travel far. When we set up our lodges that evening, the herds were very tired but still nervous.

Just before break of day another stampede took place in the same manner as before. Tracks later showed the same Real Bear caused the trouble. Another colt had been killed and other animals injured or escaped. The herd didn't run as long as they did the first time. They were brought back and separated to their rightful owners.

A council was then held by our chiefs to determine what should be done about Real Bear. Real Bear had killed and eaten parts of three horses, and caused the death or escape of many others.

[The Blackfeet believed that a form of human spirit existed within

94

the Real Bears and therefore seldom attacked them. Also, Real Bears were dangerous foes. In the past, Real Bears had killed many of their people. In those days to kill a grizzly was considered by the Blackfeet as brave a deed as killing an enemy.]

Our elders decided to move the next day, and that if Real Bear attacked the herds again, it possessed an enemy spirit and was to be hunted down and killed.

At dawn the camp moved southward. That night, as our elders had ordered, several herds were grazed some distance outward from the main herds. This was done in the hope that if Real Bear attacked again, it would attack one of the outer herds. This would allow the herd boys more time to get them under control and prevent their reaching the main herds and causing another mass stampede.

At dawn, after three suns travel, one of the outer herds was attacked by Real Bear. The herd boy shot arrows at Real Bear, none of which hit their target. Then he raced his pony after his charges and prevented them from stampeding others. Again tracks showed it was the same Real Bear that had attacked before.

When the camp moved southward that morning, several of our warriors, who owned guns [muzzle loaders obtained in trade for furs from the Hudson Bay and Northwest Fur Companies] remained behind to hunt Real Bear. Unsuccessful, they returned to camp two suns later. We were then on our own hunting grounds, one sun south of the Blood country. We moved south next dawn and set up our lodges to rest for several days.

Eight suns had passed since Real Bear had first attacked our herds. Our leaders had now decided that Real Bear didn't possess an enemy spirit but instead, a strange, evil spirit. They were sure it would attack again. Therefore, some herds were still kept in an outer circle, and as an additional protection, several small groups of mounted warriors, who possessed guns, patrolled the outer herds. My father was leader of one of these groups.

The night was clear with a full moon shining. As my father's group neared one of the herds, they heard the agonized cry of a horse. Then sounded the pounding of hoofs as the herd broke into flight. The herd boy took after it. My father's group raced to the place where the herd had been resting at the foot of a low bank, in which there was a small gully.

Upon nearing this location, they saw a movement before the gully's mouth. At their approach, they made out the form of a Real Bear in the moonlight. On the ground beside it was the body of a horse.

My father and the others fired their guns at Real Bear, which dropped to all fours and charged a short distance. Then it stopped and turned slowly in a circle as it watched the warriors, who were then riding around Real Bear firing at it as fast as they could reload. At the report of a gun, Real Bear would charge a short way toward a rider, then stop. This happened several times. The reports of the guns attracted the other groups of warriors. Just as they rode up, Real Bear lunged toward the gully mouth, dropped and died.

This Real Bear was very big. Its claws were very long. One claw was slightly deformed with a side twist. This was the identifying mark that proved this was the same bear that had attacked our horses on four occasions.

Our people rejoiced in Real Bear's death. They and our Chiefs and our Medicine Men were sure it had possessed a strange, evil spirit, since it had followed our camp for over 100 miles in eight suns's time. A Real Bear that could do this, our Medicine Men knew, was possessed by a restless spirit of great evil and destruction. Once tired of our horse herds, this spirit would then have caused greater tragedy to our people.

As near as can be determined, this bear was killed about half-way between the southwest end of the Sweet Grass Hills and the Marias River in northern Montana. Like Slaughterhouse and Old Roughhouse, this bear was a nomad. His raids, and the beliefs of the Indians, left a legend that establishes it as one of the oldest, if not the oldest, livestock-killing grizzlies on record in the northwest United States.

Grizzly Bears of Montana

WILD HORSES AND GRIZZLIES DON'T MIX

Steve Wade, a cowboy friend of mine, had an unexpected meeting with a grizzly, more than thirty years ago. Steve was running a band of wild horses at the time, in the foothills of the Pryor Mountains, a little northeast of Warren, Montana. Steve is a firm believer that wild horses and grizzlies don't mix. Steve has a good reason for his belief.

One day while riding range, he jumped a herd of twenty-three wild horses, led by a big, roan stallion. They were exceptionally fine animals, and five of them were well-marked Appaloosas. He had always wanted some Appaloosas, and since he had had some experience in trapping and running wild horses, he immediately began laying plans to catch them.

After watching them for some time, he discovered that they frequented a place he had always thought was a blind canyon. But he saw the herd enter the canyon and not return. Then he found the horses in a valley across the ridge.

One day he looked over the canyon from its rim. It was slightly curved and roughly a half-mile long by fifty feet wide. Sheer, rocky cliffs towered from seventy-five to a hundred feet high on both sides. A quarter mile from the entrance the walls narrowed, then flared out again. At the narrows were two slabs of rocks, about fifteen feet high, with a crack of a few inches between them. The slabs extended from one canyon wall to within twelve feet of the other wall. The wild ones passed through this twelve-foot gap.

Where the canyon ended in a pocket, a well-worn trail, partly concealed and canopied by scrub timber, led up through a narrow, steep-sided, rocky gully to the top of the ridge beyond the canyon. In the distant past the gully must have been an old creek bed. Within a few feet of the trail's beginning in the

97

pocket, a waterhole lay in a hollow at the base of a cliff. Half-way between the top of the hollow and the waterhole's edge lay the rotting remains of part of a tree that had fallen from the rim above. After watering, the wild ones had simply gone up the gully trail to the ridge top and on into the valley.

Barricading the gully trail with stout poles would be an easy matter. Once the herd had gone through the gap, the crack between the two slabs could be used as a slot from which to place poles extending over to the jagged rocks on the canyon wall, closing the gap. The place was a natural horse trap.

Steve cut and placed poles near the gully trail, about two hundred yards above the point where the mouth of the gully entered the pocket. He placed other poles beside the slabs at the gap. Since there was no place to hide them, the wild ones would turn back at first sight of them, but he figured that after a while they would get used to them and eventually go through the gap to water, as before.

He watched the place from vantage points whenever he could. Twice, from the rim, he saw the horse herd enter the canyon as far as the slabs, then go racing back with tails apopping. Nine weeks passed before the roan stallion allowed his charges to go through the gap. They grew more confident as time went on and nothing happened.

When the fall roundup ended, Steve quit the outfit he was working for, loaded his duffle on his pack horse, and moved to a timbered area near the canyon. He made camp and kept his string of six horses picketed on a small clearing deep in the timber. He was taking no chances on their straying away and alarming the herd which included the Appaloosas.

The wild bunch was coming to the waterhole about every third day. One night after they departed, Steve took a round-about way, so as not to go too near the canyon, and barricaded the gully trail with the poles. That night a light rain fell, which helped kill any human scent that might have been left.

The roan stallion usually led his band to the waterhole a little before sundown. About that time, two days later, Steve mounted a fast, tough buckskin from his string of horses. From an off-wind position he watched the canyon mouth from a concealed spot a short distance away.

Before long the band came into view from up the little valley. The Appaloosas stood out like a clean ace in a dirty deck. They looked grand with the setting sun shining on their hides. At the canyon mouth, they halted while the stallion tested the wind. Presently the lead-mare entered the canyon. The others followed, with the stallion bringing up the rear. The instant the herd was out of sight, Steve raced the buckskin forward. He knew what was expected of him, and made a bee-line for the entrance. Moments after entering the canyon, Steve heard the pounding of hoofs up ahead. He caught a glimpse of the herd as it dashed through the gap. They went out of sight behind the slabs. He checked the buckskin as they passed the gap, jumped off, and quickly placed the poles in position. Mounting again, he headed after the herd at a good clip. Things were surely breaking his way!

Near the end of the canyon, the buckskin caught up with the herd. They had slowed a bit, but at the sight of Steve and his horse they bolted forward. They were almost to the top of the hollow near the water hole. Steve figured they would either try to crowd into the gully trail or bunch up and mill about. He slowed the buckskin to a walk. A few yards more and he would halt and look them over.

Without warning came one sharp, whistling snort of alarm from the lead-mare. The entire herd wheeled about instantly. Two of them were knocked down. Others jumped and stumbled over them. They came straight at Steve, snorting, hoofs thundering, terror showing in their eyes. When they turned, the buckskin sat back on his hind legs. Then, as he reared up to turn about, over the back and heads of the bolting herd Steve caught a glimpse of the head and shoulders of a grizzly bear, just beyond the rotting tree. About that time one of the wild bunch collided with the buckskin. At the impact, the buckskin started to fall. Steve pulled his feet from the stirrups and jumped. A horse grazed him, knocking him sideways. Flying hoofs were all about him. He hit the ground hard and nothing gave. He covered his head with his arms. When something hit him in the side he saw the north star cut through the center of the moon and everything turned purplish black.

He was lying face down when consciousness returned. Dazed, he rolled over and gained a sitting position. Only a few seconds had passed, but not a horse was in sight. Suddenly a resounding crash came from the direction of the gully, followed by the smashing of brush. The muffled crash of breaking wood sounded down the canyon. Then all was still.

Steve got up slowly. He had several excruciatingly painful knots on his body. Directly in front of the spot where he had been lying was the outline of a horse's body in the dust. No doubt it was the buckskin's, and had been Steve's protection. The wild horses had jumped over the buckskin and also over Steve. Steve believed that in attempting to rise, the buckskin either hit him in the side with the cantle of the saddle, or with his head, and that blow knocked him unconscious.

Steve judged from the tracks that the grizzly bear was about three years old. It had probably been snoozing beside the rotting tree when the wild horses interrupted his nap. Naturally he raised up to see what the disturbance was. Since the wind was just right, the herd hadn't scented or seen him until he raised up. They were only about thirty feet apart when that happened.

As near as Steve could figure, he was knocked out about the same time the grizzly took off lickety-split for the gully trail. When the bear came to the pole barricade, he started to climb over it. The top pole must have broken under his weight and he ripped out the rest on the way down. After that, he scrambled over some boulders and tore off through the underbrush. At the gap, tracks showed the wild ones hadn't bothered to slow down for the poles. They had gone right through them. Steve found the buckskin near the mouth of the canyon. He didn't look very perky. Steve didn't feel very good himself.

"Why the grizzly picked that canyon to take his nap the same day I did to catch my Appaloosas, I'll never know," Steve said. "I never used that canyon again for anything. I don't think the grizzly or the wild ones did either."

Grizzly Bears of Wyoming

BLOODY PAWS
1889-1892

Among the outlaw grizzlies, Bloody Paws seems to hold the record for the number of domestic animals killed. During three years his accounted escapades totaled five hundred and seventy head of domestic animals destroyed, not to mention several head of wild game. The value of the stock, mostly sheep, charged to his destruction was estimated at $7,850. His boldness, and the fact that he caused the death of two hundred and sixty-three "woolies" in a single raid, were the chief factors accounting for his notoriety. Sheepman placed rewards totaling $375 on his head.

The killer's country lay considerably east of Greybull, Wyoming, and covered an area roughly thirty miles long by twenty-five miles wide. It extended from within 15 miles of the Big Horn River east to the summit of the Big Horn Mountains, and from Salt Creek on the north as far south as Paint Rock Creek. The terrain of this area varies from snow-capped mountains to open grassy stretches and timbered hills, and is well cut up by bluffs, flats, draws, coulees, ravines, and canyons. It is well watered by many creeks in the foothills and high mountains, but on the western edge the country becomes arid, almost semi-desert range.

Bloody Paws was a typical grizzly of that section of the country. He was classed as a "bald-face." He had a pale, creamy-buff coat with a slightly brownish tinge in the rolls of fur over his massive shoulders. Several times his pelage was described as of silvery whiteness.

In October, 1888, a party of trappers, on their way to their camp on Salt Creek, rode out of some timber on the crest of a low hill to discover the grizzly at the edge of a creek bottom below them. The night before it had snowed and the ground was blanketed with white. The grizzly was beside two deer that lay in a blood-splotched circle.

A noise or change of the wind which brought the bear the party's scent, caused him to stand up quickly on his hind feet for a better look at the intruders. In such a position he was in sharp profile against the snow-sprinkled underbrush and heavy timber behind him. All the men noted the bear's forepaws were drenched in blood, for they stood out conspicuously against his whitish-buff pelage.

Just as a trapper fired at him, the bear dropped to all fours. The bullet whined over his head; he scrambled to heavy timber and disappeared.

The trappers found the two deer were bucks with locked horns. One buck had been dead for some time. Unable to detach himself from his dead opponent, the live buck had been forced to remain on the spot. Shortly before the trappers arrived, the grizzly must have come upon the deer and killed the live one. The other was stiff in death and unmolested by the bear.

With the picture of the grizzly's bloody paws fresh in their minds, with his bloody tracks about them, the trappers named the bear Bloody Paws. When they returned to Greybull in the spring, they told about the bear and showed the locked horns, which they had brought along. At that time the grizzly had not been known to molest livestock and little attention was given to the affair.

During the winter the U. S. government had not kept their promises to the Shoshone Indians, and some of the younger bucks became disgruntled and bitter. In late May, 1889, several bands of braves jumped the reservation and went on the warpath, principally for beef.

Range work and the constant squabbles with raiding Indians kept the stockmen busy the first half of the year defending their property. In August, soon after the government got the Indians corraled and back on their reservation, large flocks of "woolies" made their appearance on various stretches of the public domain used by the cowmen. This caused the cowmen quite a bit of concern. Cowhands, maneuvering about the country observing the sheepman's movements, came upon five cattle skeletons, which they thought had been slain by wolves or coyotes. Later, as their hate for the sheepmen intensified, the sheepmen were blamed for the destruction.

A few weeks later, an event occurred which instantly changed their minds. A rider happened upon a cow recently killed by a bear. Nearby a calf, which had miraculously escaped the bear's attention, stood bellowing to its mother for its dinner. The rider brought the calf to the main ranch and told of his find. Bear traps were set at the cow carcass, but the grizzly never returned.

The killer struck suddenly and quickly, then traveled miles before making another foray. When he struck again near Paint Rock Creek, he was seen by a cowboy as he was leaving a horse carcass. The cowboy's description of him tallied with that of the trappers. Later on, a rider surprised the bear in the act of pulling down a cow. Although he was some distance away, he chanced a shot at the grizzly with an old Spencer rifle. He thought he hit the bear in a hind leg.

From that time, until the next year, the grizzly was not seen again. However, four more cattle were located that had been slain by him. When the fall roundup was in full swing, the bear was believed to have been the cause of a herd of saddle horses stampeding.

A wrangler was driving the horses to the noon camp so the cowhands could change mounts. As they rounded a point of timber near the camp, the horses suddenly broke and scattered. The boys at the chuck wagon saw them go. Fearing more Indian trouble, they mounted and dashed out to help the wrangler. When the herd was finally brought into the rope corral near the chuck wagon, they returned to the timber point and looked about for tracks. They found the prints of a big bear and followed them up a ravine to a boulder ridge, where further tracking was impossible. Several of the men had seen Bloody Paws' tracks before and swore the tracks found were his.

The first snow squall of the winter fell shortly after this affair. The grizzly soon went into hibernation.

When the spring thaw melted the snow, two horse traders, driving a band of horses, came upon Bloody Paws in a mountain pass. He was standing between two giant boulders in a hollow

103

just off the pass trail. When the horse herd saw him, it bolted. Before the men could dismount and reach the hollow, the bear escaped in the rock-studded terrain. In the hollow they found a freshly killed bighorn ram with a beautifully curled set of horns. Tracks revealed the grizzly had evidently seen the band of mountain sheep coming toward him. He had waited in a down wind position to charge them as they came through a narrow space leading into the hollow. Taking the ram by surprise and at close quarters, the bear brought him down before he could escape.

The ram's head was skinned out and later mounted. It, together with the locked horns of the deer mentioned above, is still in the possession of Mr. R. R. Kennofel, son of one of the horse traders.

The grizzly remained in the high country well into the summer. Indians told of finding a bighorn ewe and her lamb killed by a bear. They did not see the grizzly but their description of his enormous prints convinced stockmen it was the work of Bloody Paws.

Shortly after the Indians' report, the grizzly drifted down the mountain side into the vicinity of Beaver Creek. There it killed five calves in a meadow paralleling the stream. Several miles away, the bear slaughtered a big, muley steer. The steer had put up a terrific battle and must have seriously crippled the bear, because ever afterward the grizzly's tracks showed a decided limp. Perhaps due to this injury, Bloody Paws began to prey on domestic sheep. At any rate, soon after this he invaded his first flock of "woolies." The herder and owner, Edwin Downey, described the raid.

His flock was spread out over a rise of ground. Part were on one side and part were on the other. He was on foot at the back of the flock and couldn't see the sheep beyond the rise. Just beyond the rise a stand of lodgepole pine flanked a draw that extended out from the ridge. Suddenly the sheep dogs began barking excitedly and ran toward the draw. From the tone of their barking, he knew something was amiss. When he topped the rise, about a hundred yards below him was a big, creamy colored grizzly standing up on his hind legs. He was batting the sheep about. Every time he leaned forward, he would toss a ewe into the air with a sweep of a forepaw. Then he'd watch it with a kind of satisfied expression on his face. He was really enjoying himself. The dogs were barking and lunging at him, but he didn't pay any attention to them. Finally, he dropped on all fours and walked into the flock. The sheep just stood there blatting. Every time one got in his way, he knocked it to the ground or into the air.

Downey lined his 45-70 on him and fired. At the report, the grizzly let out a loud, growling squall and stood up. His face, head, neck, parts of his shoulders and chest were all blotched with sheep blood. He was mad. He looked all around, but didn't see Downey. Downey fired again. The bear let out a bawl and slapped at his shoulder. Then the bear started toward Downey, turned suddenly, and lit out for the woods. One of the dogs rushed the bear, but the next instant the dog went end over end. He was dead before he stopped rolling. Downey fired once more, just as the bear crashed into the brush flanking the timber, but missed him.

Downey described Bloody Paws as a "big devil" that must have been all of eight feet tall when standing up. He was certain of hitting him once, maybe twice, but the shots unquestionably were just flesh wounds. His loss was thirty-seven ewes.

Within a month the grizzly raided another flock. This caused such notoriety the story was published in several eastern newspapers.

Ford McCorkle gave me the following account of the happening, as related to him by a herder named Lowery.

Since animosity was nearing the danger point between sheep and cowmen over the rights to grazing lands, several of us sheepmen established a winter base-camp in the Big Horn River valley some distance northeast of Greybull. We figured if we had to fight, by using a base-camp we could better protect ourselves and flocks. I had one flock of twenty-eight hundred sheep, summer grazing in the mountain meadows near the head of Shell Creek. The flock was in charge of a herder named Lowery, who had a Crow Indian helper. In early fall, Lowery began driving the band toward the winter rendezvous.

Late one afternoon, Lowery camped on a flat about half a mile long on the bank of White Creek. A quarter mile back from the creek was some heavy timber. When he camped, he did not notice that the creek made a sharp right turn at the far end of the flat, to go pounding over jagged rocks as it cataracted down a bluff-lined canyon. Nor did he notice that the far end of the flat dipped sharply downward some two hundred feet to end abruptly atop a sheer seventy-foot bluff on the creek.

The flock was grazing up the flat between creek and timber. Lowery left them in the care of the Crow and went to hunt deer for camp meat. While the Crow was setting up camp, several hundred sheep moved into the ground-dip and grazed close to the bluff. From his position about the middle of the flat, the Crow couldn't see them below the crest of the dip and consequently did not know they were there.

The sharp barking of the sheep dogs from somewhere up the flat attracted his attention. At the same time a startled movement in the flock on the upper end of the flat caught his eye. All at once several sheep jumped into view from the unnoticed dip. It was then the Crow realized a ground dip lay up the flat and that something was happening in it which he could not see. As he grabbed his rifle and ran to investigate, the dogs increased their barking to a mad, frenzied tempo.

The setting sun had filled the tree tops on the distant hills with fire, and its glow cast a reddish tint over the flat and the surrounding country.

The Crow, like most Indians of that time, was superstitious. When he reached the top of the dip, he saw a compact band of about three hundred sheep near the edge of the bluff, and a reddish looking grizzly standing between him and the sheep. The bear was broadside to the Crow, in perfect silhouette against the flaming skyline. The fiery glow gave a scarlet tint to the bear's cream colored fur. The excited Crow evidently thought he was facing a red demon.

The grizzly started lumbering into the sheep, smashing at the ewes as he advanced. He would make a pass at the dogs, when they got too close, and then keep after the sheep. The sheep bunched closer together and kept backing away from the bear until they were at the bluff's edge. The Crow saw many fall off as the others continued crowding them back. The grizzly was so absorbed in the killing he never realized the Crow was near him.

Suddenly a rifle shot sounded from across the creek. The bear paused and looked in the direction from which it came. Then he saw

106

the Crow. At the same time the Crow got hold of himself, and with rifle at hip level, fired at the bear. He missed. The bear turned about. The turn constituted a short lunge toward the sheep. This caused them to jam quickly backward, and another large bunch went over the bluff. Then the bear took off for the timber at a good clip. As he did, he passed close to other sheep near the bluff. Crowding back, they forced others to tumble downward. The Crow started running for camp.

Across the creek, Lowery heard the Indian's shot. Since it came so close after his own shot, he thought it an echo. When he reached camp, the Indian wasn't there. The Crow came in later. Briefly he told Lowery what had happened, and that he was leaving, immediately. No amount of persuasion or explanation could change his mind.

The next morning. Lowery found fifty-two sheep dead or dying on top of the bluff. Two hundred and eleven others, all dead, were either at the foot of the bluff, or strung along the creek, where the current had carried them. Tracks from a limping bear showed Lowery how the grizzly had been coming up the creek along the bluff when he stumbled onto the flock and invaded it.

Several months later, Lowery met the Crow in Basin, Wyoming, and obtained the details of his part in the affair.

When the cowmen heard of the event, they laughed loud and long. The sheepmen put $300 on the grizzly's head.

A few weeks later McCorkle received a letter from a wealthy English sportsman named Dunnington, who resided in New York State. The man requested verification of newspaper accounts he had read about an outlaw grizzly. If such existed, he asked permission to bring his Russian wolfhounds to hunt for the bear. McCorkle wired him to come. Dunnington did, with pancake saddles (English Riding Saddles), eight hounds, and all the trimmings.

His dogs struck the trail of Bloody Paws in a rough stretch of country between Trapper and Paint Rock Creeks. The run lasted but a short time. When the hounds caught up with the bear, it took a stand on a huge, flat rock lying against a bank. As each of five dogs leaped to get on the rock and at him, the bear knocked them into kingdom-come. The other three returned to their master. Dunnington never saw the grizzly. He spent the balance of his stay successfully hunting wolves with the remaining hounds.

After the Englishman's departure, the bear struck twice in quick succession. Once he killed a cow and her calf. Soon after the first heavy snow, he crossed the trail of a band of elk. His footprints revealed how he had followed in their beaten path until he overtook them. The elk, ten in number, were bucking through a drift when Bloody Paws attacked and killed two yearlings. From the elk carcasses, the bear's trail led up the mountains to hibernation.

The grizzly began the year of his downfall by slaying a doe. It was found quite some distance from his den, which was located by backtracking.

Shortly afterwards, near the junction of Beaver and Shell Creeks, a cowhand came upon a range bull that had been slain by the outlaw. The bull's throat had been torn open and one of its sides caved in. Blood spots over a trampled area gave mute evidence of the battle waged there. A limping track connected Bloody Paws with the deed.

One evening during lambing season, the bear slipped up on a flock and destroyed nine ewes and eleven lambs. This flock was spread around a point of timber jutting out on a clearing. Glenn Thompson, the owner, had two Indians helping with the lambing. He had tied up his sheep dogs so as not to excite the ewes. One of the helpers, on his way to the sheep wagon, which lay just beyond the point from which they were working, surprised the grizzly at the edge of the flock. Unarmed, he ran to the wagon for a rifle. When he returned, the bear was gone.

During the next three months Bloody Paws destroyed several newborn calves. They were found at widely scattered points. One cow gave her life in defense of her young.

The last two years of his life, Bloody Paws often followed the tactics of wolves, that is, he trailed after flocks and, during the night, killed a few sheep bedded at the edge of the band. During the time of his known escapades, it is estimated he killed about one hundred and seventy sheep in this manner.

In mid-summer, northwest of Horse Creek, the outlaw made his first big night raid. The country over which this flock grazed was too rough for a sheep-tender's wagon, so the herder was using pack horses for transporting his camp equipment. This particular night he made camp in the middle of a meadow. As was his custom, he hobbled one of his horses, a mare, and let the other two graze free, knowing they'd stay close to her. He bunched the flock and unrolled his tarp (bedroll) in the center of them so he would be close to them in case of any trouble.

About midnight the herder was awakened by the barking of his dogs. A pale moon was shining. In the semi-darkness it took him a few moments to make out his dogs, and a silvery, bulky object moving up and down. With every movement came a painful, choked cry from a "woolie." Twice, spurts of fire from the herder's rifle stabbed the night; then again, as the bulky form moved hastily toward a wash crossing the meadow. Upon investigation, the herder found twenty-eight ewes dead or dying.

With coming daylight, he discovered the mare was dead. She evidently had been killed instantly by a smashing blow at the back of the head and had never issued a sound. Undoubtedly, the other horses had raced away at the bear's approach. Big grizzly tracks led from the mare to the flock. When the flock was attacked, the dogs had awakened the herder. Why they hadn't awakened him when the bear killed the mare is a mystery. Perhaps the wind was not right and the dogs did not scent the bear until the sheep began to blat from their injuries during the attack. Footprints revealed the grizzly had remained at the mare some time, eating. He had approached the mare and the flock by way of the wash and retreated the same way. Harry Kincaid, the flock owner, added $25 to the $300 reward. Before long Kincaid suffered another loss from the grizzly. This time it was from a flock of fifteen hundred sheep, herded by a Basque called Pancho. The flock was being grazed on some huge meadows that fanned out from a clearing at the base of a forested hill.

In the base of the hill was a large U-shaped pocket with a ravine running up into the woods from its rear. The sides of the U were rather steep banks. Pancho had barricaded the ravine entrance and built a low, crude brush fence across the open end of the U to make a sort of corral. Near a point on the bank above the corral, he had his camp. From this point he could look down on the entire flock, when he penned them in the U.

One evening about twilight, Pancho thought he heard a commotion in the flock. When he looked it over, nothing seemed amiss, so he returned to his campfire. Shortly thereafter he heard a sharp "blat" which he recognized as one of fear and pain. The blatting increased in volume. Grabbing his rifle, he ran to the point. His dogs bounded down the hill to the pen. From the point, Pancho saw one side of the flock was jammed against the brush fence. Between the other side and the ravine lay a broken line of dead and dying sheep. A cream colored grizzly was smashing at every "woolie" within its reach as it advanced into the flock.

The bear was in the shadow of a bank and with dust and the fading twilight, he was difficult to see. Bloody Paws was nearly in the center of the flock when Pancho fired. The bullet hit him in the rump. With a bawl of pain, he spun about, started a dash in that direction, then stopped short at the foot of the bank below Pancho. There he stood up and looked around. Pancho shot again. The bullet struck a forepaw. The bear grabbed the paw in his mouth, then released it. Opening and closing his jaws in sullen rage, he continued looking about.

As he dropped to all fours, Pancho fired and missed. A light wind was blowing from the bear to the herder and consequently the bear did not scent him. The grizzly began going around in a circle, smashing every "woolie" he came to, trying to locate his antagonist. He never once looked upward.

About this time the dogs reached the pen. They scrambled over, under, and around the sheep as they made for the bear. Pancho's fourth shot again struck the grizzly in the rump. With an enraged "woof," the bear came to a half-standing position, then broke and ran for the ravine. A spurt of dust showed Pancho's next shot was a clean miss. The dogs pursued the bear into the ravine, but soon came back. Forty-eight ewes lay dead or dying in the corral. Kincaid added another $50 to the standing reward.

For a long period the outlaw was not heard from. The sheepmen hoped he had died from the effects of Pancho's bullets, but such was not the case.

South and east of Shell and White Creeks lived a halfbreed Shoshone Indian, whose true name was Dono Oso (Shoshone for Buffalo Robe; he was also known as Jack Madden). Buffalo

Robe had established a small cow outfit. His range lay in a saucer-like basin surrounded by bluffs. He had built a cabin, stable, and set of corrals where a narrow canyon led into the basin. He lived there with his wife and three children. It was said, but never proved, that Buffalo Robe had relied on his long rope, fast horse, a running iron, guts, and luck to establish his herd. At any rate, he had a good start of cattle and a fine herd of horses of which he was very proud. One day he found two dead colts with big bear tracks about them. Buffalo Robe had seen Bloody Paws' tracks and knew from these prints that Bloody Paws had been the killer. He spent several days in an unsuccessful hunt for the grizzly. Then, suddenly, he met the bear one afternoon.

Buffalo Robe was riding a spirited horse up a ravine trail leading to his cabin. Bloody Paws was coming down another trail leading through another ravine. The two trails joined at the foot of a hill. A few yards from the junction, Buffalo Robe's horse pitched suddenly, throwing him to the ground. The horse turned and ran back down the trail. When Buffalo Robe gained his feet, the first thing he saw was Bloody Paws. The bear was at the junction of the trails and about thirty feet away. Buffalo Robe's rifle was in its scabbard on the fleeing horse. He drew his .44 Colt and fired at the grizzly. With a snarl, the bear charged. Buffalo Robe put four more bullets into the grizzly. It staggered and dropped less than three yards from him. One of the bullets hit the bear over an eye and passed out just back of the ear, tearing out part of the brain pan.

As Buffalo Robe dressed the bear, he found three aged bullet scars put there by the Basque, and five fresh wounds from his own .44. He showed the hide to the sheepmen, who gladly paid him the full reward, for Bloody Paws was the most notorious sheep-killing grizzly of the time.

Bloody Paws was estimated to have been twenty years old and to have weighed close to 1000 pounds. All through life the grizzly was referred to, and thought to be, a male. Upon the bear's death, it was discovered to be a female. She was never seen or known to have been with cubs, and was undoubtedly barren.

Grizzly Bears of Wyoming

OTHER WYOMING GRIZZLIES

In addition to the famous Bloody Paws, three other Wyoming livestock-killing grizzlies had a price on their heads. Although much detail of their activities is lacking, a few accurate accounts were available.

Southwest of the Bloody Paws domain lay the Owl Creek Mountains, with its eastern jut known as Blue Ridge. It is a short range and in 1893 was scarcely traveled. Small outlaw bands of Shoshone, Crow, and Arapaho Indians, together with some white rustler gangs, prowled the territory. None helped the honest stockmen. In that district a light brown-colored grizzly appeared. A southern cowhand named him Old Rebel. For five years he roamed and killed cattle at will. He was intensely active in the region around the headwaters of the South Fork of Mud Creek. A reward of $275 induced a couple of discharged soldiers to hunt him down and collect the cash.

East of the Teton National Forest, a brownish-buff marked grizzly, named The Butcher, or Butch, spent the years between 1896 and 1900 raiding horses, cattle, and sheep belonging to outfits in the valley and foothills between the Gros Ventre Range and Wind River Mountains. The bear was hunted unsuccessfully many times by professional hunters. It slew $4500 worth of livestock. A $375 reward on the bear's head was never paid. The bear disappeared in the fall of 1900 and was not seen again. It was believed to have either died of old age, or that a slide covered its den during hibernation, preventing its escape.

Bighorn Whitey was a giant, grayish, almost-white grizzly. From 1904 to 1908, he raided livestock on a stretch of the Big Horn Mountains near the head of Buffalo Creek, northwest of Badwater, Wyoming. He was killed by a Burlington Railroad survey crew who shared the $200 reward given for his destruction.

An eye witness account of a grizzly killing an elk on Specimen Ridge in the Yellowstone country is related by Forest Ranger W. M. Rush. He had been assigned to watch game movements and had selected a sheltered spot against a white-bark pine tree halfway across a long snowfield about a hundred yards from an elk trail:

A half hour more and the first of a long single file of elk appeared. There were nearly a hundred of them. Almost every cow had a calf trailing closely behind her. They followed the well-beaten trail made by old bulls and cows that had survived winter in the mountains. The path was deep, rough and narrow, and the cows moved slowly, adjusting their gait to the faltering walk of their little ones. At the edge of the snowfield, the leader stopped to muzzle her calf. After a moment the little one followed her, and behind them another pair, and another, until the string extended halfway across the snowfield, plodding silently in the icy ruts.

Without warning a great furry ball of grizzly bear hurtled out of the forest into the middle of the moving line. The terror stricken elk tried to run but they could not. Some of them jumped to one side of the beaten trail. Their sharp hoofs cut through the crusted snow and they floundered helpless, unable to go further. Some crawled on top of those ahead in the trail, piling up in a frantic heap. Others turned and tried to go back. Panic held them in a milling throng while the bear picked out a cow that had fallen on her side. With a swift rush the grizzly was upon her, grabbing her nose with a long-clawed paw while it sank saber-like teeth into her neck and ripped open her belly with the other front paw. It was over in a matter of seconds and the bear paid no more attention to its kill. It turned and hurtled itself on a bunch of elk that were jammed in the trail, seized a calf in its mouth, and made off with it across the snow, disappearing again in the shadows.

This story is an exception. I repeat again my conviction, gained from years of research and observation, that grizzlies as a whole decline to do their own wild game killing.

Grizzly Bears of Colorado

OLD MOSE
1882-1904

By Janet Sterling

Ranchers living in the Black Mountain country near Canon
City never tire of telling stories of Old Mose, a grizzly bear
killed on Waugh Mountain near the Stirrup ranch fifty-six years
ago.

Old Mose roamed the stockmen's land, tore down their fences,
killed thousands of dollars worth of cattle and even killed their
friend. He was credited with being one of the largest grizzlies
ever killed in the Rocky Mountain Empire.

J. W. Anthony of Indiana killed the bear April 30, 1904. He
owned a pack of thirty well-trained bear dogs. It was with the
help of his dogs that he was able to track Old Mose to his death.
He was visiting at the Stirrup ranch, then owned by the late
Wharton H. Pigg.

Killed shortly after coming out of hibernation, Old Mose was
not as heavy as he was known to have been in other seasons. At
that, he weighed 875 pounds, hog dressed. A clipping from the
Canon City *Record* at that time says: "The skin of Old Mose
measures ten feet four inches in length and nine feet six inches
across the shoulders."

Anthony's luck in killing was due to a meeting with Wharton H.
Pigg, who had tracked Old Mose almost constantly since he first
saw his tracks in 1882.

Old Mose was named by Pigg and Henry Beecher, old-time
ranchers, who gave him his name after a notorious bear that
used to range about Flat Top Mountain in Routt County and was
killed in 1882.

Old Mose's large tracks identified him on his periodic visits.

After he lost a toe and part of another from his right foot, they were more easily distinguished.

Old Mose must not be confused with Old Four Toes, killed in Montrose county in 1903, who was considered at the time of his death the largest grizzly bear ever killed. The skin of Old Four Toes was displayed at the St. Louis Fair and measured about twelve feet in length, but its width was sacrificed to gain its length.

Although Old Mose lost his toes in a lake at the foot of Black Mountain years ago, they were kept by Beulah Beeler Evans and since her death have been in possession of relatives on the Beeler ranch near Fairplay.

Wharton H. Pigg, for years a representative of the United States Biological Survey and a noted hunter and writer of animal stories, was also on the lookout for Old Mose. A man of the mountains, he learned much of the bear's cunning and knew that he ranged from Tarryall creek to the Cochetopa range, with Black Mountain about center of it. The bear covered his territory about every thirty days.

By close reckoning Pigg figured the time the bear would be in the Black Mountain vicinity, and sent one of his men to set a trap. The trapper, knowing the bear's habit of bathing and his cunning in avoiding traps in the brush, set one in the lake where his tracks had previously been seen leading to the water.

One morning a small boy, John Douglas, was sent to scout the trap set, and carried back the news that Old Mose was in the trap. Several men grabbed their guns and headed for the lake. They found Old Mose had gone, but that he had left two toes in the trap.

Old Mose was seen many times and was always reported to be of unusual size. His kills proved this. He would kill cattle of any size and on a single ranch he killed three full-grown bulls, one a five year old registered Hereford. It is a matter of conjecture what his weight might have been if he had been killed in the fall.

Pigg found a number of Old Mose's dens. These were always on the north side of a hill in heavy timber where the snow lay deep all winter and where he would not be far from water. In the Colorado country a grizzly goes into hibernation usually in November to remain until April. Smaller bears sleep longer as a rule and more soundly. A grizzly sleeps lightly and any warm spell is apt to rouse him.

For many years Pigg followed Old Mose from feeding ground to feeding ground. Always Old Mose evaded him as well as his hunters.

Pigg found many of his warm beds and by them learned more of his cunning. Old Mose, upon resting, would make almost a complete circle of great diameter, leaving a small place untrampled. This was done in case anyone was following his tracks and if the wind changed during his slumber, he could make his get-away through the untrampled part. While his eyesight was poor, his scent was keen and was his best way in evading his enemy.

Dr. E. G. Lancaster of Colorado College examined the brain of Old Mose and said it was one of the most interesting he had ever examined on account of its size and position. It was almost six inches long and weighed but fifteen ounces. The brain ratio was only 1-1000 for Old Mose as compared with the ratio of a man's brain to his body of 1-45.

"Two centers of the brain were enormously developed—smell and hearing—and despite what any hunter may say, he never did much thinking!" said Dr. Lancaster. "He was cunning, not intelligent. It was all instinct with him."

The crimes laid to Old Mose were many, and ranchers were wont to say he killed more cattle than Watkins ever thought of stealing. (Watkins, a cattle thief, was hanged for his crimes on the First Street bridge in Canon City years ago.) But the greatest crime ever placed upon the bear was the killing of Jake Ratcliff of Fairplay, Colorado.

It was in the fall of 1883. Ratcliff, together with Hank Seymore and another companion, went out to hunt Old Mose who had been killing cattle near Black Mountain. Several days later the men made camp for the night on the north side of Ratcliff gulch. The bear's tracks and one of his kills, still warm, had been found nearby, but they could not find the killer himself.

Early the next morning each of the three took a different trail.

A shot was to call the others in case they should come upon their prey.

There was no breeze to carry the scent of the hunters. Shortly after Ratcliff left his companions he went down a gully where he noticed a pile of fresh dirt. He thought someone was prospecting and walked over to the hole. It proved to be the place Old Mose had chosen to hibernate. Old Mose was near and saw Ratcliff.

Ratcliff was brought to a sudden stop when he came on the bear but a few yards away. Ratcliff aimed and fired hastily. The bullet pierced the bear's shoulder, but the gun was a small caliber and he failed to kill him with repeated shots.

For a moment Old Mose shook with pain and rage. Then, making for his assailant, he grabbed him and threw him in the air. Ratcliff, torn and bruised, fell on the ground still conscious.

For awhile Old Mose stood near sniffing and grunting angrily. Ratcliff lay still for what seemed a long time. Not hearing the bear any more and suffering intense pain caused by the bear's claws, he raised his head ever so slightly. Old Mose, still close by, saw the movement and bounding back grabbed Ratcliff and again threw him on the ground. This time Ratcliff did not move and Old Mose walked away.

Ratcliff's companions found him unconscious. They improvised a stretcher from a camp blanket tied to aspen poles and carried him back to camp.

Ratcliff rallied briefly and told the men his story. One hunter went to a nearby ranch for help and returned with R. M. Pope and R. W. Foster, who assisted in cutting a path through aspen thickets until the party reached Flemming's ranch.

A doctor was summoned, but it was too late. Ratcliff's scalp was almost torn off, his side crushed and his back cruelly cut. He did not survive.

Old Mose was hunted more than ever. Many traps were set, but the old bear avoided them. Somehow he knew if they were set or sprung, and if sprung, he would help himself to the bait. If set, he would circle the trap and go on his way.

G. A. Hall, a cattleman living near Fairplay, made a trap by building a pen three feet high with a gap in it. A dead cow was placed in the pen and a steel trap set in the gap entrance. Old Mose robbed this pen three times but was never harmed.

C. W. Talbot met him on Beaver Creek. His tracks were found on Gribble Mountain and on the Stirrup ranch. He remained on the Dave Walker ranch above Guffy for almost a week. A horse had been killed by lightning in a pasture surrounded by a stake and rider fence. Several nights Old Mose went to the pasture for a feed and each time he chose a new entrance by knocking down the fence and walking through the break.

John Lyle, riding along a mountain top a year before Old Mose was killed, saw the grizzly wandering below him. Lyle aimed at him and was sure that one bullet struck the bear in the back. He heard the bear give a cry of pain and surprise. Lyle told this to his friends. One happened to be Pigg.

When Old Mose was dressed, Pigg found the bullet lodged in the backbone and found a vertebra nicked. The bullet had been fired by someone above the bear, at an angle of 45 degrees, a corroboration of Lyle's story.

Several bullets were found in the carcass, some fired by Ratcliff.

As the hide was hung up in Wright & Morgan's market in Canon City, a slight scar was noticed on one of the bear's hips.

"Let's cover that up," Pigg advised, "for every fellow who sees it will claim that he made it."

The scar was carefully concealed just before Dan Hall walked in carrying an umbrella.

"So you got him," Hall remarked. "I took a shot at him one time up on Table Mountain and hit him, too. I was close enough to know. I remember I hit him right about there on the right hip." Hall raised his umbrella and almost touched the spot so recently covered. The scar was creditably attributed to Hall.

To Wharton Pigg goes the credit of killing a probable mate of Old Mose on Cover Mountain a number of years before. Pigg ran across the she-bear and a yearling at the headwaters of High creek. He killed them both.

Old Mose was killed about four miles from the Stirrup ranch, then owned by Pigg, which is about thirty-five miles northwest of Canon City.

Anthony and Pigg, with a pack of nine dogs, were camped at

118

the ranch of Ed Simmins near Dick's gulch. Tracks were found near the ranch on their first day out. They followed the trail for three days before the dogs struck a fresh track. Old Mose had been eating a cow and then going into a nearby thicket to rest.

Because he was recently out of hibernation, nature did not allow the partaking of much food at one time. The stomach, contracted, did not hold much more than five pounds. Consequently, he did not go far from his kill.

The dogs were excited and ran about sniffing at the edge of snow patches. Anthony followed a pack of four dogs and Pigg the other five. In this way they became separated.

Pigg had had ear trouble which caused a slight deafness. He did not hear the furious barking of the dogs that had at last found their prey. Anthony, however, did hear and ran to the dogs.

Anthony's account follows:

"I soon came upon the dogs in a grove of quaking aspen where they surrounded the biggest bear I ever saw in my life. At first he took no notice of me, and paid little attention to the dogs while he walked along, though they were pulling fur every minute. I fired at about seventy-five yards. Then I let go three more in succession, all of which were hits, but none fatal. He stood on his haunches and looked at me, dropped down and started for me.

"At about three yards I took careful aim with my 30-40 Winchester. At this distance bears generally make a rush upon a man.

"I got him between the eyes and he fell without a quiver. It took seven men to get him to the Stirrup ranch and we figured he weighed close to 1000 pounds."

Besides killing Ratcliff, Old Mose was supposed to have killed James Asher, whose mutilated body was found in a place frequented by Old Mose between Canon City and Salida. The bones and the booted spurs of a cowboy were found by a party of prospectors on Thirty-nine Mile Mountain in Park county. They were found in a cave showing tracks of this enormous bear.

For a long time the hide of Old Mose hung here and there in Canon City until Anthony took it to Indiana, but the memory of its beauty and size is still told by local hunters and ranchers.

Grizzly Bears of Colorado

OTHER COLORADO GRIZZLIES

Colorado has a host of outlaw grizzlies. Some of their careers were short-lived. A few of these renegades prowled the ranges for several years. The most notorious were Old Mose, Three Toes, Old Four Toes, and Club Foot. They roamed in Routt, Rio Blanco, Eagle, Montrose, and Grand counties from 1882 to 1908 and were terror to ranchmen among whose cattle they created great havoc.

Of the four bears, Old Mose was the only one to carry a cash reward on his head, and the only outlaw grizzly known to have killed a man. The reward of $100 was the lowest on any outlaw grizzly, an incongruity in view of the fact he took a human life.

Three Toes gained his name when he left two toes in a bear trap. Club Foot lost half a foot in the same way.

Old Four Toes was considered the largest grizzly ever killed in Colorado prior to 1905 and one of the largest outlaw grizzlies ever killed. His weight was a little less than 1,100 pounds. His skin measured twelve feet in length. He ranged in Montrose county for years prior to the time he was killed. His pelt was on exhibition at the St. Louis Fair and drew large crowds among the mid-westerners and easterners who had heard of, but never seen, a grizzly, or its pelt.

Another account of a Colorado cattle-killer appeared in the Denver *Times*, September 7, 1900. The bear, although unnamed, became well known in a short time because of its destruction of livestock over a wide area. The bear was a monstrous silver-tip. It had been living on the best grass-fed steers of the Rio Grande Valley for many years. Ranchmen of Mineral county had long suffered from the depredations of this particular bear. Many strenuous efforts were made to find the bear and kill it, but the grizzly had proved too cunning.

Four beautiful, adult grizzlies, coming into the feeding grounds in Yellowstone National Park. *Photo courtesy of National Park Service, Yellowstone National Park.*

A happy, aged grizzly, poses for his self-taken picture while feeding on the bait that was tied to the camera trigger by a fine wire. *Photo courtesy of David de L. Condon.*

"You again! Can't you leave us tired fellows alone?" *Photo courtesy of David de L. Condon.*

The fine head and shoulder picture of this bear, who perhaps was thinking, "Whatch'a doin'?" was made as it looked questioningly at the photographer. *Photo courtesy of David de L. Condon.*

Photography can be so tiring! *Photo courtesy of David de L. Condon.*

A dark color phase of the grizzly. This bear's blackish-brown pelage is rare in the Wyoming country. *Photo courtesy of National Park Service, Yellowstone National Park.*

A dark, buff colored grizzly, and two lighter colored ones, moving onto the feeding grounds to wait for the Park rangers to give them their dinner. *Photo courtesy of National Park Service, Yellowstone National Park.*

Three color phases of grizzlies: darkish-brown, medium brown, and buff. Note raised shoulder roach on bear in center. Grizzlies of Idaho, Montana, and Canadian Provinces have dark pelage similar to the bear at the extreme left of the picture. *Photo courtesy of National Park Service, Yellowstone National Park.*

This grizzly was out of hibernation but a short time when this picture was taken. The bear was nearing the feeding ground at Yellowstone National Park. Note the long, last winter fur, and the gauntness of the flanks and rib area. *Photo courtesy of National Park Service, Yellowstone National Park.*

"Did someone call?" *Photo courtesy of National Park Service, Yellowstone National Park.*

This night picture, taken in the fall, when bears put on fat to carry themselves through their long winter sleep, was made from a camera-blind. Moments after the flash the bear turned and ran off in the brush. Upon departing, if he could have spoken, he probably would have said, "I didn't mean to do it! I only ate the bait!" *Photo courtesy of David de L. Condon.*

Winter was fast approaching when the grizzly killed a cow and calf. The next day he brought down a steer. Knowing the bear occasionally returned to its kills, "Dolph" Lust, of the Galloway ranch, moved one of the carcasses near a group of trees and stood guard. During the night he heard a rustling in the brush. He pulled up his Winchester. The sounds ceased. Then he heard a deep snort and the bear swiftly moving away. It had winded the hunter.

Light snow was falling the next day. Lust started out with his dogs and found fresh tracks leading from one of the slain animals. In a short time the dogs brought the bear to bay, but one venturing too close was killed by one blow. Lust put a couple of balls into the bear, enraging it all the more. As it started after him, Lust shot it in the neck, then ran for tall timber. While running, he fastened his gun to his cartridge belt with a piece of twine. He needed his arms free for climbing, but did not want to be caught in the air without a weapon.

The bear was giving him a close chase. Behind the bear came the dogs, yelping and snapping. One dog finally grabbed a hold on the bear. While the bear stopped to attend to the dog, Lust scrambled up a spruce tree. From astride the first strong limb, Lust opened fire on the bear. At the first fresh wound it renewed its chase. As the bear came toward the tree, Lust continued to fire. Weakened but undaunted, the bear reached the foot of the tree and tried to start up, but grizzlies cannot climb trees. Lust drew a bead on the bear's head and pulled the trigger. The great arms relaxed from around the tree. A streak of blood ran down the bear's forehead as he fell backward and lay in death agony. Lust slid down the tree and put another bullet into the grizzly. The livestock killer of the Rio Grande valley would kill no more.

Lust came back to the spot later with some pack mules to carry his prize to the ranch. The handsome hide of the silver-tip was taken to Creede where Lust gave it to a friend to use on the floor of his library.

Grizzly Bears of New Mexico

NEW MEXICO GRIZZLIES

At one time New Mexico had a heavy grizzly population. It rapidly declined with the settling up of the country. A few years ago, T. Vernon Bailey, New Mexico wildlife conservationist, estimated less than fifty grizzlies within the boundary of the state in 1917, and that most of them were gone by 1928. Among the early population were several notorious outlaws.

Renegade was mainly a sheep and goat killer. His range was on the west slope and at the southern end of the Chaska Mountains. He preyed upon flocks belonging to reservation Indians and slew enough cattle and horses belonging to independent stockmen to warrant a $460 reward for his hide. No reward was paid, however, because he was finally brought down by a government hunter in 1915. Renegade was the last of the notorious outlaws to go.

In the northern reaches of the Datil Mountains, New Mexico, lived a killer grizzly the Navajo Indians called The Phantom, or Ghost Bear. They told many tales of seeing him from nearby ridges, only to have him completely disappear before they could get within accurate shooting range. The Phantom was taffy colored, with frosty-white tipped hair over his shoulders and back. He wandered over a wild, broken country with many canyons and arroyos in which to hide.

This bear began his career by playing havoc with several trail herds. In 1888 the section was a haven for rustlers and desperados of all sorts. Because of this, sheep and cowmen were too busy guarding their interests to make an organized hunt for the bear until 1890. After that time he was trailed repeatedly.

While hunting some horse thieves in fine falling snow, Cliff Black, a stock detective, came upon the Phantom's tracks. He followed them to the mouth of a short pine-studded canyon, hastily circled to the canyon's head, and waited the bear's approach. The grizzly soon appeared on an open slope about one hundred yards away. Black fired three 45-90 slugs into the bear's body before it collapsed. The pelt was sold to a hotel man in Santa Fe for $100. Black also collected the $200 reward posted for the bear's destruction. Between 1887 and 1892, The Phantom destroyed livestock valued at approximately $4000.

Another prominent New Mexico outlaw grizzly was known as the Raider. He ranged between the Saddle and Moggolan Mountains near the present town of Reserve during the years between 1877 and 1881. He destroyed many cattle and gained notoriety because of his night raids on grazing horses and mules belonging to freight-wagon caravans. Freight line stock was constantly close herded by the teamsters and mule skinners for fear of surprise attacks by Indians or Mexicans. The grizzly invaded them regardless of the presence of man. On such an occasion, he was shot at by two Mexican teamsters. The next morning his body was found a short distance away. Wicks and Hickman of San Antonio, Texas, a large, long-distance freighting company, through their agent at Las Cruces, New Mexico, paid $200 to the two men for Raider's destruction. Several stockmen contributed $250 more.

In the foothills of the Animas and Hatchet Mountains roamed a notorious nomadic stock-killer, Old Clubfoot. The bear often returned from forays to dominate the ranges east of the town of Rodeo, New Mexico. Old Clubfoot was hunted down by the famous predatory animal hunter Ben V. Lilly, who trailed the bear from New Mexico into Chihuahua and Sonora, Mexico, then north into Arizona.

In northern Mexico, New Mexico, and southern Arizona lived a species of grizzly locally referred to as the Desert Grizzly. They roamed the stretches of semi-desert flanking the foothills of the various mountain ranges of that region. These grizzlies were mostly light in color with a slightly darker marking down the back. They averaged about 650 pounds in weight.

In the spring of 1913, Ben V. Lilly was hunting on the ranges of people who were paying him bounties for bears and lions in Alma Section, New Mexico. That year he killed 48 bears and lions, about an equal number of each. The snow stayed on late that year and the bears killed a great many cattle. On the third day of April, Lilly bagged his largest grizzly. The bear measured nine feet from the end of his nose to the end of his tail, eight feet around the body, and four feet eight inches in height. The hind foot was twelve inches long, measuring along the top side; skull eighteen inches in length; ankle fourteen inches around, both rear and front. From the size of this bear, it must have weighed more than 1000 pounds. Lilly stated he wanted $1000 for it; however, he contributed the hide to the museum at Washington, D.C.

Grizzly Bears of Arizona and Nevada

ARIZONA AND NEVADA GRIZZLIES

Arizona

In the Chuska Mountains of Arizona ranged a dark-grey furred grizzly that the stockmen named Apache. He was a sheep and goat killer. Many of his attacks were upon small flocks handled by Indian herders. The bear took few victims in each flock, but they totaled heavily over a period of time. The rough terrain over which he roamed made hunting him difficult and probably extended his life span. Apache destroyed between five and six thousand dollars worth of domestic stock during the six year period between 1905 and 1911. He was trapped and killed by a packer who received the $180 bounty for him.

Nevada

Nevada had two outlaw grizzlies. One ranged in the southern part of the state along the Eldorado Mountains near the north rim of the Grand Canyon, just south of Searchlight, Nevada. In 1895 this area, as now, was sparsely populated, but the grizzly raided roaming flocks of sheep and herds of cattle whenever they entered his domain. He killed many deer, mustangs, and some bighorns.

The Paiute Indians named him The-Evil-Spirit-Bear-Who-Lives-in-the-Rocks, and told many tales about him. It seems an Indian, while hunting on the rocky ledges of the Colorado River Canyon, was killed by the bear. The stockmen called the bear Paiute. He was brought down by a party of mustang runners in 1899 at a chance meeting. They collected $225 which had been placed on his head.

At the other end of the state, just north of the Bull Run Mountains, lies the Western Shoshone Indian Reservation. A little east of it are the headwaters of the Bruneau River. Between the Bruneau and the Owyhee River to the south, lies a wild, broken country of gashed land comprising part of the Owyhee River breaks. In 1898, and for several years before and after, this area was the hideout and rendezvous for gangs of rustlers who stole cattle and horses from stockmen in Idaho, Nevada, and Oregon. It was also the home of Slaughterhouse, a stock-killing grizzly that had nomadic tendencies.

During the long, hot summer months, the creeks and rivers of this area dry up leaving but few water holes. The bear spent much of his time around these water holes, preying upon bands of wild burros and wild horses that inhabited the breaks, as they came to water. Several times the grizzly was "jumped" and shot at near watering spots. On one occasion he was known to have been injured.

Long before his appearance in the break country, stockmen and Indians reported having seen him miles to the northwest, in the vicinity of the Targhee National Forest, Idaho. The bear left a trail of dead cattle and sheep along his route of migration between the two districts. For two years thereafter little attention was paid to him. But when he drifted south and began killing livestock grazing at the north end of the Humboldt River Valley, stockmen quickly took notice of him.

In arid sections of country, livestock hold fairly close to water courses. The grizzly's boldness increased as he penetrated deeper into the livestock domain down-river, and the reward for him grew to a considerable sum. Only during the last four years of his life was a record kept of his kills. During that time he accounted for two hundred and fifty-four sheep, forty-one head of cattle, and nine horses.

Slaughterhouse was blackish-brown in pelage, with shaggy fur, and weighed around 825 pounds. Unlike most grizzlies of the southern Idaho-northern Nevada section, he was carnivorous and turned out to be a violent assassin by habit. Since the country was sparsely populated, buzzards, coyotes, bobcats, or wolves usually led someone to his kills. With such a lapse of time be-

134

tween kill and discovery, a successful hunt for him was next to impossible. Twice professional hunters were employed, but the grizzly's hide-and-seek tactics, in a country of plentiful cover, meant only defeat for the hunters. When trailed with dogs, he always escaped. Always after being harassed, he returned to his rendezvous in the breaks. His wariness and caution in detecting traps were uncanny. Poisoned carcasses proved futile, for he was never known to eat of flesh other than that of animals killed by himself.

Nine years after his first presence was known, Slaughterhouse was destroyed by the late Charles Foley of Reno, Nevada. At the time, 1907, Foley was employed by a sheepman as a camp-tender packing supplies to various sheep herders. One morning soon after sunup, as his string of pack mules entered a narrow arroyo near Silver Creek, the grizzly emerged from a cross-arroyo to attack the mules. There was a brief, wild mix-up within the confined quarters. One mule was killed and another viciously clawed on the neck and shoulders. Then the bear charged Foley. From his rearing horse Foley fired five 30-30 slugs into the bear. It dropped a few yards from him.

How many wild burros and wild horses this outlaw destroyed in the break country will never be known. From reports it can be safely assumed the number ran over one hundred head. If an accurate record of all of Slaughterhouse's kills were known, there is little doubt that it would place him as the most destructive outlaw grizzly of them all. He was generally unknown and unheard of because of his remote range in the breaks. Bounties totaling $523 were collected by Foley from cattle and sheep men. The latter contributed the most because Slaughterhouse was decidedly a sheep-killer.

Grizzly Bears of Utah

RED ROBBER
1880-1885

The earliest authentic and verifiable record containing details of a livestock-killing grizzly with a reward on his head appears in 1881, although his activity began in 1880.

The bear was named Red Robber because he ranged over a territory in southeastern Utah, just east of the notorious and historical Robber's Roost country. This particular area was a hideout for rustler gangs operating from Canada to Mexico during the 1880's and early 1890's.

The Red Robber, weighing about 900 pounds, was larger than the average grizzly of his locality. He was considered a color freak. His long hair was rusty red with a buff-yellow stripe, about six inches wide, running down the center of his back from mid-neck to rump. The tips of his hair were frosty white.

His range covered a somewhat triangular plot of ground between the Green River on the west, the Book Cliffs on the north, and with the Colorado River forming the southeast side of the triangle. He was known to have killed cattle south of the Colorado River, in the area north of Elk Ridge and the Abajo Mountains east of Hatch Wash. His whole domain was a maze of small plateaus, cliffs, bluffs, canyons, and rough rocky draws, with water holes between rivers miles apart. All of the terrain was covered with bunch-grass, sage, and scrub cedar, typical semi-desert range, with timber and grassy meadows on the high points and in the surrounding mountains.

The JRX cow outfit, owned by James Riley, was located to the south of the Book Cliffs, near the Colorado River. A cowhand employed by Riley found the evidence of the Red Robber's first known raid. One spring morning he heard cattle bawling beyond a low rise. Across the rise he came upon four longhorn cows

136

bawling themselves hoarse. Another, with deep claw-marks on her blood covered face, head, neck and shoulders, was standing spraddle-legged, head down with a broken horn. The ground was torn up and sprayed with blood for yards around. Close by, he found five dead calves. All had crushed skulls or bodies. One had been all but devoured. Bloody bear tracks led from the massacre to a rocky, scrub-cedar covered ridge, where the cowhand lost them.

On arid rangelands, watering places are too far apart for young or newborn calves to travel to them. Several cows will often leave their calves with one cow (sometimes a steer or bull) to guard them while they go to drink. Upon returning to their calf rendezvous, the cow that stood guard then goes for a drink while the others watch her offspring. Unquestionably, the grizzly had come upon such a rendezvous and after battling the cow on guard into helplessness had massacred the calves.

Cowmen in that section of the country had enough trouble guarding their stock from roaming bands of Southern Ute Indians and rustling gangs operating from the rugged, canyon country of Robber's Roost, without a grizzly adding to their woes.

A few days after the massacre, another rider found a steer killed by the bear, and a small band of Utes reported two more killed. Riley and some men set out to hunt down the killer. Buzzards circling over a meadow led them to a dead yearling. The Utes claimed it had been dead about three days and had been killed by wolves. Grizzly tracks at the carcass corresponded in size with those found at the calf massacre. In this instance, however, there was little doubt that the bear had come upon the yearling after the wolves had killed it. The animal had been hamstrung and its throat had been slashed. Wolf tracks and uneaten parts of the carcass were scattered about under nearby bushes, all indicative of wolf work.

The bear's tracks were fairly fresh, so the hunters followed them. Trailing was slow and difficult. The bear often moved over rough terrain which the men on horseback had to circle. Near sundown the party emerged onto a ledge paralleling a deep side canyon leading to the Green River. They stopped to look down the side canyon at the turbulent waters of the Green, far below. Suddenly, a quarter of a mile in front of them, a big, rusty-red grizzly with a buff-yellow stripe along its back came lumbering between two points of scrub cedar.

All the men shot at the bear before it disappeared behind a jut of rock, but no hits were scored. Realizing it would be dark before they could reach the spot where the bear had disappeared, and next to impossible to follow him in the maze of draws, crevices, and side canyons flanking the river, the party gave up the hunt.

Within a month, six friendly Utes rode into the JRX ranch and told Riley a bear had attacked fourteen wild horses they had left overnight in a horse trap. Riley and some of his men went to the trap. It was located at the end of a small blind-pocket canyon. The Utes had barricaded the narrow entrance with a log gate. The trap itself was small and surrounded by high, sheer, rocky walls. The Utes had caught the herd the afternoon before and then gone to their camp for the night. Upon returning to the trap next morning, they discovered the bear had invaded it during their absence. Three horses were dead. Two others were so badly injured they had to be shot. One was a beautiful blaze-faced chestnut that Riley had tried several times to capture. Riley was so angered he vowed vengeance on all bears, offering $50 to anyone who would bring him the Red Robber's hide: the first reward placed on the bear.

Claw marks on the log gate told how the grizzly had climbed into the trap. The battle had been fast and furious: ripping, tearing claws against flying hoofs. Both bear and horses used savage, flashing teeth. The corral was a mass of blood, pieces of horse hide and flesh, and a few hunks of bear hide with rusty-red fur attached. Despite the battle, the bear had eaten his fill before departing. He left a bloody, limping trail. The men, figuring he wouldn't travel far, followed his tracks until dark. At break of day, they were on the trail again, but lost it in a rocky descent leading to the Colorado River.

No one was known to have seen Red Robber again that year, although several head of stock recently killed by him were found by Utes and men in Riley's, and other cowmen's, employ.

In April, 1881, on a flat near Hatch Wash, Ed Rowe, a cowhand drifting through the country, came upon a big, dun-colored longhorn steer sprawled at the base of some boulders. From the evidence, it had made a fighting stand against a bear. The steer had a good set of five-foot horns. One horn was smeared with blood several inches back from the tip, and both horns had claw and tooth marks upon them. The steer's neck and shoulders were a mass of shredded flesh. One side of the lower jaw was crushed and almost bitten in two. The steer soon died.

Although he had heard no noise when nearing the flat, Rowe knew from the bear's tracks that he had almost ridden into the middle of the grizzly-longhorn feud. Bushes had been beaten to the earth over a large section of the flat. The ground was mangled, and a fine film of blood was sprayed over the embattled area, indicating a lengthy fight.

Rowe's horses were nervous and kept looking toward the mouth of a nearby, brush-lined draw. A fresh and bloody trail led that way. Rowe circled to a point and scanned the draw. He was just in time to see a rusty-red bulk disappear where the draw turned abruptly behind a hill. He trailed the bear to a jumble of brush-lined gullies. It was unsafe to follow farther but having heard of Riley's $50 reward, he spent the rest of the day scouting in the vicinity for the grizzly. That evening he camped near the steer. The grizzly did not return. In the morning, Rowe cut the clawed horns from the steers skull and took them to a ranch east of Hatch Wash. He told of the grizzly incident and left the horns. They were nailed over a corral gate. Years later they were mounted and hung in a saloon in Gallup, New Mexico, where I located and bought them in 1935.

Seven more head of stock, known to be Red Robber victims, were found south of the Colorado River. By late summer the grizzly struck north of the river at various places on his triangular range. His kills enraged the stockmen. By that time it was more than clear to them that he was killing just for the sake of killing. Often he never devoured any part of the animal he destroyed. His known escapades at that time accounted for forty-two head of stock. Three ranch owners placed a reward of $150 on his head.

Soon after the fall roundup, a cowman, referred to in the records only as Long John, was trailing a herd of steers from his ranch north of the Book Cliffs to Gallup, New Mexico. Long John moved south along the Green River for some distance, then he cut overland southeast to the Colorado River. The night before crossing the river, he camped on a small plateau at the head of a canyon leading down to the Colorado River. On two sides of this plateau were stands of timber with a line of low cliffs close behind. The remuda was grazing at a point where the cliffs and the timber stand ended. The herd was on the plateau, encircled by the rim of the Colorado River Canyon, the remuda, the camp, and the line of cliffs, which were almost half a mile away. Soon after dark the moon began to play hide-and-seek with the drifting clouds. A little later the nighthawk (night horse wrangler) noticed the remuda was becoming nervous. Knowing horses scare easily, he kept circling them in an attempt to determine the cause of their restlessness. As the wind changed, the remuda drifted toward the timber.

Just as the wrangler started to turn back the remuda, he saw a big grizzly come out of a shallow gulch, only a few yards from him. A horse saw the bear, too. It let go a whistling snort of alarm and bolted. The others followed at top speed, racing toward the bedded herd. Just then the moon went behind clouds. Pitch darkness blotted out everything.

As the remuda dashed into the herd, the cattle stampeded toward the timber at the base of the cliffs. The boys on guard tried to get the herd into a mill, but failed. The night was a bedlam of crashing brush, clanking horns, yelling men and bellowing cattle. When the melee ended, three steers were found dead, having broken their necks in collisions with trees. Five were tramped to death, and three had broken legs and had to be shot.

Cowmen of the vicinity were having ever increasing trouble with rustlers, as well as with thieving bands of Utes. To protect their interests, they formed a Stockgrower's Association. At their initial meeting, November 18, 1891, an entry in their brand and record book reads: "Brother Long John upon returneth from Gallup saith Red Robber stampedith herd north of Colorado causing 11 loss. Stock killed to this date 53. Reward subscribith $150 to $300 on grissel."

Throughout 1882, the grizzly was seen just once. A Ute surprised him feeding on a yearling. Armed with only a bow and arrow, he sent two arrows at the bear before it escaped into a wooded canyon. One arrow hit the outlaw in the back.

In the course of the year, from kills reported, stockmen were able to trace the bear's movements over his triangular range. His first kills appeared north and east of the confluence of the Green and Colorado Rivers. From there they spread northward in a zigzag course across half of the triangle to the base of the Book Cliffs. After that, they were found eastward to the Colorado River, then south throughout the other half of the triangle. Red Robber reached the Green River in late fall. The cowmen calculated the bear was hibernating either in the Orange Cliffs or in the rocky walls of Stillwater Canyon through which the Green River surges to its junction with the Colorado. During the year the outlaw was known to have destroyed an additional thirty-four head of cattle, three horses, and two colts. This brought his known kills to ninety-two animals slaughtered up to that date.

That fall the Association added another $100 to the reward. They also hired a professional hunter named Zack Crabtree to hunt the bear down. Zack had attained fair success in the Choiskai Mountain region of northwestern New Mexico.

During the winter, stories came out of the Robber's Roost saying that several outlaw gangs were having a private war of their own, due to their stealing each other's stolen cattle. This proved to be true. From time to time, well mounted and heavily armed men were seen traveling in groups. Lone cowhands, employed by honest cattlemen, were ambushed and shot at. One was killed and another seriously injured. The situation became so bad that cowhands began traveling in pairs.

Utes told of a two-day pitched battle west of the Green River on the north branch of Barrier Creek near Red Dome. The rival gangs had employed Ute help. Two Utes, four white men, and a Mexican had been killed in the fight, with several injured.

In the spring of 1883, the Association did not tell Crabtree of the outlaw's feud. Instead, they supplied him with a friendly Ute as camp tender and hustled him to a point near the mouth of the Green River to await Red Robber's appearance. Before long they found the grizzly's first known kill of the year. On the third day of tracking, someone shot at Crabtree from a grove of trees. From his Ute helper he learned of the outlaw situation. He quit, ending the hunt for Red Robber for the time being. During the year the bear was known to have killed nineteen more cattle, although he was never seen. No doubt the grizzly killed many more during the season, since much of the territory over which he roamed was not penetrated unnecessarily by the stockmen because of the rustlers' feud.

The next spring no kills by the Red Robber were found. The stockmen hoped the bear had died during the winter. Their hopes were short-lived. In the early summer a band of Utes told of coming upon the grizzly south of the Colorado River near Elk Ridge. The bear remained in that district for some time and was known to have killed several cattle.

On two occasions, when the grizzly's victims were discovered near the ranch of a man named Noce, a group of cowboys spent several days hunting him, but their efforts were wasted. The grizzly always escaped into draws, gullies, or small canyons whenever they attempted to close in on him. They did kill a two-year old grizzly they chanced to come upon. By late summer the Red Robber crossed the Colorado River and preyed upon stock belonging to Riley and another cowman named Woodruff. Only one incident of his boldness came to light in that year of 1884. At a small Ute hunting camp the grizzly suddenly appeared from a stand of scrub cedar, charged a band of horses grazing close by, and killed one. The Ute bucks were all away hunting, but one of the squaws fired at the bear with an old, smoothbore gun, hitting him in the left shoulder. The grizzly charged the squaws. They fled. Upon reaching the camp, his charge stopped. He vented his wrath on camp items, tearing up everything he came in contact with. After this event, the bear's left forepaw track showed a limp, probably caused by the wound in its shoulder.

When winter settled down, the grizzly hibernated and the stockmen listed their yearly losses from him at twenty-seven head. They added $75 to the general reward, plus an additional $75 if the bear were killed by any professional hunter who desired to hunt for him. Their offer brought results. Just before spring broke in 1885, a hunter named Claude Schinlinn arrived at the Woodruff cow outfit with a pack of hounds, to await the bear's appearance. He never had a chance to try his luck on the grizzly.

When the snow began to melt, two aged prospectors named Parson and Monrow, with their pack burros loaded with supplies, returned to their mining claim. They had staked and worked the claim, located at the southwest end of the Abajo Mountains, the year before. Also, they had built a cabin. The back half of it was built into a bank; the front was made of big, flat stones. The roof was of poles covered with brush and dirt. They had left several deer hides in the cabin during the winter. With the warmth of spring, the hides gave off a strong odor. This apparently attracted the grizzly's attention. When the two prospectors approached their cabin, they were startled to see the Red Robber in the act of tearing a hole in the roof. The wind was blowing from the bear toward them and he had his back turned to them. The men got within thirty yards of him and opened fire. Both shots drove home. The grizzly, with a growl of rage and pain, reared up as he turned around. He stumbled backward, stepping into the hole he had torn in the roof. The miners put three more bullets into him before he freed himself and scrambled from the roof. He charged, not at them but at one of their burros. Parson took careful aim and fired just as the grizzly knocked the burro to the ground. The slug broke the bear's spine just back of the shoulder. The bear dropped, turned, and dragging his hindquarters, tried to charge the miners. He died only seconds later.

When the men skinned the grizzly, they found two aged bullet wounds, which told them the bear had been wounded by unknown parties, possibly rustlers, at one time or another. They also cut out an arrowhead imbedded in its back. The ball from the squaw's smoothbore gun was extracted from the left shoulder muscle. Many scars were also on his head, neck, chest, and sides, unquestionably received in battles with longhorns. They collected the $475 Association reward, plus $50 from Riley for the hide.

A few years later, Riley sold his interests in Utah and bought a ranch in the Datil Mountain country of New Mexico. There, until 1907, the grizzly's skin adorned the floor of his ranch office.

Such was the end of the stock-killing career of the Red Robber. From 1880 to 1885 he had killed, or caused to be killed, one hundred and thirty-eight known head of livestock, valued at about $3500. Over half of them he had killed wantonly, with no part of the animal having been devoured.

Grizzly Bears of Idaho

OLD SILVER
1898-1901

The grizzlies of the Idaho country, as said earlier, feed on vegetation, fish, ground squirrels, and other small rodents. Seldom do they partake of rotten or freshly killed animals or do their own killing of larger animals.

The record of livestock destruction by the grizzly in Idaho is practically nil. The names of several "would-be-livestock-killers" came to my attention, but in the final run-down only one, Old Silver, turned out to be an outlaw in the true sense of the word. His activities accounted for the destruction of thousands of dollars worth of livestock.

After two years of Old Silver's ruthless stock-killing, Gus Linquist, an old-timer in the vicinity, was hired by cattlemen to hunt the bear down. Failing after several tries, he attempted to trap him. Placing traps at localitites the animal frequented proved futile. No matter how cleverly they were concealed, Old Silver circled about them. Finally, Gus selected a small hollow with a narrow entrance between huge boulders. Over the boulders lay a fallen tree covered with a thick growth of berry bushes. The tree and bushes prevented any large animal from entering the hollow from above. Gus killed a horse in the hollow. Then he cut it up so the scent would carry well and placed one bear trap beside the carcass and another one in the narrow entrance.

Two days later he found a black bear caught in the entrance trap. Old Silver had escaped again. His tracks led to within five yards of the entrance, then rounded the boulders and went on to a meadow where he had killed a heifer. The fact that the black bear was alive, and other signs, was proof the grizzly had come and gone before the black bear had arrived.

Old Silver was never known to return to a kill once he had left it. Like most grizzlies in the Idaho country, he was never known to eat carrion.

A homesteader named Swenson, and his wife, upon returning by horse and buggy to their homestead, surprised Old Silver in a corral in which he had slain a calf. Swenson killed the outlaw grizzly and collected the $200 which stockmen had pooled as the reward for him.

Old Silver tipped the scales at nine hundred eighty-four pounds. He was a magnificent fellow with dark, bluish-gray, almost black, pelage. Silvery-white tinged the tips of the hair over his shoulders and along his back.

From 1898 to 1901 he ranged along the west and east sides of the Middle Fork of the Salmon River, from Rapid River at the southwest end of the Salmon Mountains as far north as Wilson Creek on the west slopes of the Yellowjacket Mountains. He was particularly active throughout this district on range lands just west of the Salmon and in the territory beween Loon and Camas Creeks, east of the river.

Grizzly Bears of Idaho

OTHER IDAHO GRIZZLIES

Pete Henry, a professional hunter and trapper, was employed numerous times by stockmen throughout Montana and Idaho. Later he served as a government hunter. He related an experience to me in which a grizzly was blamed for a lion's work.

In 1911 Pete was sent for by a stockman running cattle on summer range in the mountains northeast of the North Fork of the Clearwater River in the vicinity of Pott Mountain. He took four hounds along, striking out by pack horse from the vicinity now known as Pierce, Idaho. At the outfit's camp he met the owner, foreman, and two cowhands. They told him the grizzly had killed three cows and two calves within the past six weeks. From a ridge, the foreman and owner had seen the grizzly at one of the carcasses, and they were convinced it was the animal killing their stock.

Pete spent a day looking over the kills. All five were at different places in two meadows separated by a timbered ridge. The hounds turned up several old and two recently killed deer carcasses. All were within a mile radius and with the deer kills, everything pointed to lion's work. Due to the small area, Pete thought the lion was a female and had kittens in a den somewhere close by.

A few days later a freshly killed heifer was found with grizzly tracks about it. Pete looked the carcass over. Although the tracks of a fair-sized grizzly were about, other signs told him a lion had broken the heifer's neck. The bear had taken only a few bites out of the carcass. Pete knew grizzlies of that section seldom killed livestock or deer. In his opinion, the grizzly was ranging in the locality and when it scented the dead heifer, followed its nose, as it had done once before when it was seen at a carcass.

Pete led the hounds in a big circle around the heifer, but they could not pick up a tracking scent.

The next morning he started to make a half-mile circle around the carcass. In a draw on the ridge, the hounds gave tongue and raced up the ridge. As the run went on, the baying grew more excited. Pete felt sure it was a female lion, trying to hold close to her kittens. About noon the baying changed to sharp barking, indicating the cat had come to bay. He shot the lion out of a tree growing out over a pile of boulders. It was within a quarter-mile of where the hounds had jumped her trail.

She was a husky female, weighing about 130 pounds. Her kittens must have been born late in the spring, for she was still heavy with milk. One of the hounds was a good cold trailer, so Pete tried back-tracking her, but a heavy thunder shower came up and destroyed the scent. The den was never found.

In Idaho, one early fall afternoon in 1897, three cowhands came upon a steer which they judged had been killed less than an hour before. They were near the head of Little Lost River, between the Lost River Mountains on the west and the Little Lost River Mountains on the east. The steer had been frightfully clawed and its throat torn open. Big grizzly tracks led from it over a ridge to a creek. The men fanned out along the creek and cut for tracks, which they soon found and followed to a small clearing. There they jumped the grizzly. It immediately ran toward heavy brush and trees close by. All three men shot at the bear. Blood spots assured them he had been hit. The men penetrated the forest a short distance, but down-timber and underbrush on a rugged slope blocked their progress and turned them back.

The cow outfit's superintendent, Ticon, had come from the east a few years before and had learned a bit about the cattle business. In some unexplained way, he had been hired as managing-superintendent of the outfit, which was owned by a group of Englishmen residing in Ottawa, Canada. The owners had imported eight purebred Hereford bulls from England to breed-up their range stock, a herd of crossed Durham-Longhorn blood.

Ticon knew little about the cattle business and less about grizzlies. Upon hearing that a grizzly had killed one of his em-

148

ployer's cattle, he issued an order for two men to stay on the grizzly's trail until it, and any other bears they came upon, were killed. He also stated he did not want any of the company's valuable stock slaughtered by grizzlies.

The imported Herefords were the first known to have been brought to that section of the country and were, no doubt, an expensive investment. But the slain steer was a crossed Durham-Longhorn. At the time it was killed, all eight imported bulls were being kept in a stout corral at the main ranch. The experienced cowhands couldn't see the logic of Ticon's instructions, but orders were orders.

The next day two riders returned with dogs and took up the grizzly's trail, but lost it where it forded Little Lost River. They spent two weeks hunting throughout the surrounding country. During that time they killed three adult grizzlies and a six months old cub. Then the dogs struck the trail of a big grizzly, which the hunters believed to be the steer killer. The dogs kept on the trail from mid-morning until late afternoon. They brought the bear to bay at a cliff base beside a meadow. He was a big, dark-ish-brown, grey fellow. When the riders approached and dismounted, he charged them. They put four heavy slugs into him before he dropped. A recent bullet wound high upon his rump and another in the fleshy part of his back gave reasonable assurance he was the steer killer they had previously wounded.

In all probability the grizzly encountered the steer at close quarters, possibly was charged by it, and killed it in the fight that followed. No part of the steer was eaten by the bear. The grizzly had killed but one known critter, nine miles from where he was slain. Without doubt the steer was killed in a chance meeting, but orders issued by an inexperienced, and reputedly vain, conceited, and egotistical superintendent cost the lives of four other magnificent and guiltless animals which, with few exceptions in that territory, are known to be non-carnivorous. No other cattle in the district were known to have been killed by grizzlies yet hunters and stockmen had seen many of these bears throughout the territory for years.

Grizzly Bears of Washington

WASHINGTON GRIZZLIES

In Washington from 1900 to 1903, a grizzly known as Crippler, or Old Crip, harassed stockmen to the cost of over $6000. The Crippler was blackish in color with long, grayish-tipped fur on his neck and along his back. His left foreleg from mid-shoulder down was a silvery-gray, making him easy to distinguish. Because of this marking, on some occasions the bear was referred to as a pinto. He was seen several times fishing in streams and was shot at three times near cattle kills. His tracks indicated he deliberately stalked his prey, killing without cause. He seldom ate a victim. Because he was not a big bear, as grizzlies go in that section, many cattle that he attacked escaped. Some lived, but most of them had to be done away with, when stockmen came upon them. His crippling tactics accounted for his name.

The Crippler was first seen in 1900, when about two years old, at the north end of the Chelan Range. Later he moved eastward into Okanogan country. He established a territory of his own in the Methow River Valley, which stretches south from Lost River to Chewak Creek. Much of his activity is vague. During the winter it was believed he hibernated at the head of Wolf Creek in the Chelan Range. He was killed on Wolf Creek by a packer named Edar Olsen, who was carrying supplies to a party of timber-cruisers camped northwest of the Chelan Range. No set reward had been put on the Crippler's head, but individual stockmen posted $210 which was paid to Olsen.

Just east of Mt. Rainier National Park another Washington stock-killing grizzly raided herds between 1887 and 1889. He was never named and much data about him is lacking. His forays began late in life. His domain spread north and south of the Naches River in the vicinity of its junction with the American River. His estimated toll of stock was placed at fifty head plus an inaccurate count of elk, deer, and mountain sheep. His fur was a grayish-black. He was between eighteen and twenty-five years of age when an unknown freight-wagon driver killed him and collected the $200 bounty.

Big Blue was a stock-killer of considerable note. He roamed in the foothills of the Blue Mountains east of Walla Walla, Washington, from 1897 to 1900. He destroyed deer and elk, over two hundred sheep, and sixty-four known cattle. The $150 reward for his blackish-gray hide was paid to a Nez Perces Indian who shot him dead when he charged a band of cayuses in the Indian's care.

A grizzly bear invaded the cattle ranges of the north-central part of Washington in 1952 and was killed by a predatory hunter. It was thought that the bear entered the state from Canada. The Washington State Department of Game regards the grizzly bear as a menace to the cattle-raising sections of the state.

In 1954, the Department of Game of the State of Washington estimated that there were only ten grizzly bears in the state, chiefly confined to a small region in the very northeast corner. Three were killed during the hunting season of 1952. In the ten years prior to 1954, the kill averaged about one a year. In Washington, the grizzly bear is classified along with the black bear. In the eastern part of the state they can be killed from the first of September to the first of November.

Grizzly Bears of Oregon

THE BANDIT
1899-1904

In the late spring of 1899, Pete Houx was driving a herd of three hundred half-wild, crossed Longhorn-Hereford cattle from Rock Creek in central Oregon to his ranch in the beautiful Wallowa Valley, in the northeastern corner of the state. One afternoon as the herd reached a point near the town of Elgin, a mountain storm suddenly swept toward it from the Blue Mountains which flanked the herd on the north and west. Between the herd's position and the Wallowa Valley, which sat at the foot of the Wallowa Mountains to the southeast, lay the head of the Grande Ronde River elbow, a ten-mile strip of rough, broken country which Houx had yet to cross before reaching his ranch.

Because of the oncoming storm, Houx immediately went into camp. Leaving the cook with the chuck wagon, he rode for the herd, which was some distance ahead. When Houx arrived, the men had the herd bunched on a flat at the base of a low ridge near a grove of pines. The sky overhead had turned blue-black; to the north it was a pale yellowish-gray. The air was sultry hot and so still you could hear a mouse breathe.

Pete scattered the men about the herd, knowing the coming storm and half-wild cattle were a perfect setup for a stampede. No sooner had the men taken position than a strong ground wind sprang up from the northwest. A few minutes later the whole herd threw their heads up in unison and looked toward the north.

A big grizzly topped the ridge near the pine grove. He stood up on his hind legs and looked the herd over with cool deliberation. The bear made a perfect silhouette against the low, yellowish-grey skyline. All the men saw him, but none dared to shoot for fear of starting the "spooked-up" cattle into a run. Suddenly the grizzly dropped on all fours and disappeared behind the ridge. Then lightning slashed the sky and the heavy rain hit.

The grizzly must have circled the cattle three times before leaving the vicinity, for on three occasions the entire herd stopped moving, faced the west, and slowly turned their heads toward the north as they continually sniffed the wind. The bear was probably circling in that direction and the cattle were following his movements by scent. While the bear was to their south and east, the herd just walked and milled, always nervous. This was the first known appearance of the future cattle-killer of the Wallowa district.

The outfit crossed the Grande Ronde the next day. They camped that night on its eastern bank at the upper end of the Wallowa Valley. The herd fed and bedded down. At midnight two riders from the chuck wagon relieved the two on guard. Things seemed peaceful. Suddenly the cattle jumped to their feet. They did not run, just stood still, blowing and sucking in air. The men on guard hastened to a point at the head of the herd. Across from them a cow issued a terrified bawl of pain. Another bawled a moment later. Seconds passed. The riders made out a commotion going on among the cattle in the direction from which the bawling had come. They circled the tense cattle. Just as they saw the form of a bear in the moonlight, the herd stampeded. The riders forgot the bear and took out after the herd. Day was breaking when they and the boys who had ridden out from the chuck wagon had the herd together and milling.

Houx and one of his men returned to the place where the stampede began. Upon approaching the spot where the bear had been seen, they found three dead cows. All had broken necks. The milk bags of two had been eaten, as well as part of the hind-quarter of one. The men began tracking the bear. Near a timber-spur extending out on the valley from the elbow breaks, they caught up with him as he was about to enter the woods. Both men shot at him. At the revolver reports he spun around, bit at a spot near his right shoulder, and then with a loud growl disappeared in the underbrush.

Both men had a good look at the grizzly and were sure that the bear's face about the eyes and nose was a decided white color, and that the rest of his body was a dark, bluish-gray with whitish hair on his great shoulders. Because of the masklike markings on his face, he became known as the Bandit.

A month passed before the Bandit was heard from again. A line rider, at the northeast end of the valley, discovered the partly eaten carcass of a steer covered with grass, branches, and dirt. The carcass was watched for several days, but the bear did not return.

The rest of the year, various cow outfits suffered losses by the grizzly. All animals found either had their skulls crushed or their necks broken. With coming winter, the grizzly worked southward on the east side of the valley. Soon after the first snow he hibernated.

At a local stockmen's meeting, a checkup revealed that since the grizzly's first activity in the valley he had destroyed sixteen head of stock. However, no reward was placed on his life at that time.

Rod Denton told of the next known encounter with the Bandit. In the spring of 1900 he came upon the bear unexpectedly while driving some pack horses to a summer fishing camp in the vicinity of the headwaters of Sheep Creek, on the east slope of the Wallowas.

The ground was slippery under melting snow. The pack string was about to make a turn at the top of a small, rock gutted ridge when the lead horse whistled and shied off to one side. It tried to turn about, slipped, and fell. The others snorted and scattered in alarm. A downed tree prevented a full view of the trail ahead, but when Rod's own mount issued a snort of alarm and reared up, he caught a brief glimpse of the whitefaced grizzly, mouth open, tongue out, standing in the center of the turn, looking quizzically at the panicky horses. Rod fired his 30-30 as his horse reared again. The shot went wild. The horse made a half-turn and started sliding down the loose rocky slope. By the time Rod got him stopped and the other horses together, the grizzly had gone.

Tracks revealed the Bandit had retreated down the opposite side of the slope to the protecting shelter of some heavy timber. Rod followed the tracks for a way. When they entered a tangle of blow-downs that lay criss-crossed so heavily the tracks were hard to follow, he wisely gave up the hunt. By back-tracking, he located the place where the bear had hibernated. The den was under a large fallen tree on the edge of a draw near timberline. The tree trunk at that point was five feet above the ground. Against its wide spread roots, the bear had dug out a hollow three feet deep, five feet in diameter, and bedded it with dead leaves and parts of the rotten roots.

While examining the den, he sensed something behind him. He turned, and across the draw was the Bandit beside some boulders, intently watching him. Before Rod could shoot, the grizzly tore off behind the boulders. While Rod had been tracking the grizzly, the bear had circled the wooded slope and followed him.

A few weeks later, beside Sheep Creek, a cowman named Dorgan found a half-eaten elk which had been killed by the grizzly. After that, until late fall, the bear left a trail of death and destruction wherever he went. Shortly before the Bandit began his winter sleep, he killed an expensive Shorthorn bull that had only recently been brought to the section by a man named Scott. That fall, because of other stockmen's losses, which totaled twenty-one head for the year, the cattlemen placed a reward of $150 on the killer.

During the first half of 1901, the Bandit did not penetrate the valley.

A party of Indians, returning from a salmon-spearing trip on the Snake River to the east, told of seeing the bear beside a doe which they believed it had killed. One claimed to have shot and hit him in the hump over his shoulder. Other Indians had seen a bear with such markings in the Umatilla Mountains to the west a few years before. Increasing population had undoubtedly driven him eastward. Because of this first known locale, he was sometimes referred to as the Whitefaced Bear of the Umatillas.

About mid-summer, the Bandit moved into the south end of the valley. He killed several cattle before moving northward a few miles. One night he entered a line camp corral on the Old Martin ranch and attacked some horses. The melee that followed awoke two cowhands stationed at the camp. They came out of their cabin in time to see the bear climbing out of the corral. The grizzly was straddling the top corral log. He fell forward and went sprawling to the ground. In the semi-darkness the men were fearful of hitting a mare, so they waited until the bear was clear of the corral before shooting. They fired three shots, but none of them was effective. One horse was dead and another was clawed along the back from neck to rump and had to be shot.

Cowmen had various line camps scattered over their ranges for feeding and caring for weak and sick stock throughout the winter. In summer, hay crews cut the wild hay near the camps and stacked it for winter use. Late one night at such a camp near the Houx ranch, the Bandit attacked a mixed band of mules and horses as they grazed. He downed two mules and critically injured a horse. The animals were all work stock and unattended. No member of the hay crew was awakened during the attack by any animal's cry, if any was issued, although the slain animals were but a short distance from where the men slept.

Houx was very proud of three black and tan hounds which he used to hunt mountain lions. The next day, after several false starts, he succeeded in getting them to trail the grizzly. The run lasted half a day. The hounds were far in the lead when Houx and two others heard their stacatto-like barkings, indicating that the bear was cornered. Their barking came from a rocky, timber-studded canyon about a mile and a half ahead. By the time the men entered the canyon the barking had stopped. Beside the canyon creek they came upon three dead hounds. All were strung out along the bank a few yards apart. One had a crushed head; another a broken back and caved-in sides; a leg and shoulder of the third hound had been completely torn off. Tracks showed the bear had come to bay on a gravel bar under an overhanging rock. When he moved from the bar he had killed each hound as it had rushed to attack him. Houx donated $100 to the reward, bringing the total to $250.

With the first cool nights of fall, the killer showed up at the mouth of a grassy, timber-fringed canyon leading to meadows high on the east end of the Wallowa Mountains. In this location he made successful raids on critters drifting down from their summer range in the meadows. The Bandit had accounted for twelve head of cattle when cattlemen decided to take time to hunt for him. But they never saw him. While hunting him near the canyon, he moved north and west to the vicinity of the present Wallowa Lake. In that area he invaded a hunter's camp while its occupants were afield, and pulled down and ate most of a dressed elk that had been hanging from a tree.

After the first snow, the bear returned to his old haunts on the east side of the valley, killing ruthlessly whenever he desired. With his increased activity, he became bolder on each foray. Twice he killed animals within rifle shot of ranch houses. On another occasion he charged into a band of mares with young and killed a colt. An Indian lad in charge of the band raced his pony toward the nearest ranch to report the happening. On his way he met two cowhands who immediately returned with him. At the colt carcass, they found the grizzly had departed to the security of heavy timber nearby and made good his escape.

At the year's end the Bandit had destroyed twenty-four more domestic animals. The reward was increased to $500.

The year 1903 was the grizzly's most destructive, and his boldest invasion of the ranchers' domain. By mid-summer his ventures accounted for twenty-six spring calves and four cows. With such slaughter going on, ranch owners organized three groups of five men each, and laid out a plan to hunt him. The groups were located at vantage points throughout the district in which the grizzly was thought to be at that particular time. The groups were to be notified immediately of the next kill of the grizzly. The nearest group would try to track the bear while the others would circle about to likely spots where the bear might go. In this manner they hoped to encounter the Bandit and put an end to him. It sounded reasonable and they felt it might work.

Before long, a steer was discovered that had been dead only a few hours. One group closed in and started trailing the bear. A rain during the previous night made tracking easy. The trail led to a densely timbered and brush covered ridge. The group took a short cut through draws and ravines to a valley beyond the ridge. They expected to pick up the trail at a boggy spot bears were known to frequent, but they found no grizzly tracks there. Later developments indicated the Bandit must have sensed he was being trailed, for he had doubled back on his route and escaped.

Several nights later he killed again, far south of the bog. He entered a large corral at the headquarters of a ranch and killed nine weaner-calves and badly mauled several others, escaping before the act was detected. Only a small part of one calf was eaten.

Two hundred cows and their calves had been run into one corral early that morning. During the day the calves were separated from the cows and placed in an adjoining corral. A lane for hay ran between the two corrals. Soon after being separated, both calves and cows began to bellow—the cows for their calves to come to them and the calves for their dams to come to them so they could suckle. This is a common weaning practice used by some cow outfits. The bellowing goes on continually for about two or three days before the cows are released. The hungry cows immediately drift back to the grassy range lands. Cowhands also see to it that they move far from the calf corral. During the separation, feed racks in the cow corral are empty, but those in the calf corral are kept full of hay. The calves, being hungry, soon learn to eat the hay, and two or three days after the cows are released, they are turned loose to roam the range.

The Bandit may have been attracted by the noise, investigated, and killed for the lust of killing. His victims' cries were lost amid the bellowing and undetected by the boys in a bunkhouse nearby.

While the name of the ranch was unrecorded, a news item stated that George Weatly added $100 to the standing reward for the Bandit.

While awaiting the fall roundup, eight cowhands spent the rest of the summer unsuccessfully hunting for the grizzly. Before the bear took his winter nap, he destroyed several more cattle and three mules; yet no one had seen him during the year.

In 1904, as usual, the outlaw became active soon after the snow began to melt. His first victims were deer which were found in the foothills. Later, a mare was found slain and frightfully clawed. Close by her was the partly devoured carcass of a colt. Two trappers baited and set traps near the carcass. One trap was a dead-fall that black bears sprung and tore up. Within the next four months nineteen head of livestock were destroyed by the killer, twelve being spring calves.

In the fall, at the edge of a timber-fringed meadow, two coyotes led to the discovery of a gelding that had been killed by the Bandit. The horse had entered a small indentation in a low bank to drink at a spring. Tracks revealed the grizzly had come in behind the horse and had killed it with a smashing neck blow as it attempted to dash by him in the narrow opening.

The gelding was a well-trained roping horse belonging to a cowboy named Charley Logue. The loss of the horse was a tough one for Logue who had just started a small outfit of his own in the Wallowa foothills. He immediately set out to hunt the grizzly, calculating the reward would compensate for the loss of his horse as well as help with his ranch, which was begun on a nip-and-tuck basis.

In ten days time he never so much as saw one of the grizzly's enormous tracks. He was well up in the Wallowas when the first snow storm forced him to take cover for a day. A foot of snow was on the ground when he started down the mountain side. About half a day's ride from his ranch, he emerged from a point of woods and into a clearing that sloped gently downward. The air was still and the sky, red with the afterglow of sunset, cast its soft purplish-rose hues over the snowy hills. Near the center of the clearing, his pack and saddle horses stopped abruptly and looked intently ahead. Scanning the timber that lined the meadow, he was electrified to see a big grizzly tearing chunks of bark from a rotten log in front of a stand of bushes at the timber's edge. It had its back to Logue, and was so engrossed in searching for grubs that it had not heard his approach.

Visibility was bad, but Logue drew his 45-70, took aim at the center of the grizzly's shoulders, and pressed the trigger. The bear issued a bawling-growl, started to raise up, then flopped forward. It lay still for a moment, then thrashed wildly about and finally relaxed. Logue waited some time before approaching the bear, rifle always ready. When he saw the whitish markings on the face, he knew the Bandit's career was over.

Just as Logue shot, the grizzly had looked up and the heavy slug, only grazing his shoulder, had smashed into the point where the neck joins the head. He was killed instantly and his actions afterwards were the result of nerve reaction.

159

The next day it snowed again, but Logue and some of his friends took a team and sled and brought the Bandit to the little town of Joseph, Oregon.

The Bandit weighed over 1000 pounds. He had dark, beautiful thick fur, with a grayish tinge on the tips over his neck, shoulders, and along his back. The white hair, which gave the impression of a mask, extended across his face at eye level and a short way down his nose. He was judged to be about fifteen years old.

His stock-killing activities were confined to the north and east sides of the Wallowa Valley, although he killed wild game inhabiting the mountainous area as far south as the headwaters of Sheep Creek at the east end of the Wallowa Mountains. In his lifetime he was known to have killed one hundred and forty-five head of domestic livestock, forty-eight of which were calves or colts. The dollar value, at that time, of all stock destroyed by the big grizzly amounted to $9000.

When he was skinned, a scar showed high on the hump of his left shoulder, confirming the Indian's claim of a hit three years before. Several pieces of a shattered bullet were cut from tissues along the grizzly's right shoulder, where Houx and his men hit him the first time the bear was seen in the valley.

Throughout the five years of the Bandit's reign, the Wallowa Valley was nearly all owned or leased by big cow outfits. It was not settled as thickly as it is today, although there were more outfits and people in the valley than in nearby areas of comparable size. In such a small area as the Bandit covered, it had been comparatively easy to account for his actions. He had been seen on several occasions and the mystery to cattlemen was how the bear existed so long.

At a barn dance, given by the cattlemen, the bear was barbecued and Logue given the $600 reward. He had the bearskin made into a rug and kept it for many years.

Grizzly Bears of California

CALIFORNIA GRIZZLIES

The grizzly bear was mentioned in California history from the time the first Spaniards invaded the territory. Although there are many recordings of their livestock destruction, only a few stories go into any detail.

The California grizzly was the largest and most ferocious of the species, and there are many accounts telling how they mauled, and in many incidents, killed Indians, explorers, vaqueros, trappers, '49ers, and settlers that followed them.

Despite their long history in the state, there are only a few records in which they attacked man without cause. Usually one will find the great bears were first deliberately set upon by those attacked, injured, or killed.

The Spanish settlers, to their sorrow, encountered the grizzly upon their arrival. The great bears dealt them destructive blows from the time they took up their grants of land on which to graze herds of cattle, horses, sheep, and goats. The bears raided vine-yards, orchards, and livestock, with no respect for property and with practically none for the Spaniards themselves. Many old transcripts reveal that sheepherders drove their flocks to open meadows and built fire barriers around them at night to ward off marauding bears.

Whenever a Spanish don took up a grant of land in the valleys or the mountain foothills, it wasn't long before the grizzlies abounding in the mountains commenced their raids on his stock. To guard against them, each evening the vaqueros drove the stock away from the timber along the creeks and the foot of the mountains, out into the open valleys. Several vaqueros kept watch all night. Regardless of this precaution, sometimes during the night the bellow of some unfortunate bullock was heard, followed by the rush of his companions.

By daybreak the vaqueros were in the saddle, and the bear, gorged with his feast, was overtaken and stretched out with a reata around his neck and each foot. Then one of the riders, making fast his reata to the horn of his saddle, and trusting his horse to keep it taut, would dismount, and with his knife dispatch the helpless bear. In some areas as many as a hundred grizzlies were destroyed before they were driven back into the mountains, or learned no longer to molest livestock.

Old Mission parchments disclose how the grizzlies took heavy toll of their stock. However, their raids were so hit and miss that only a few accounts mention a stock-killing grizzly becoming so notorious that a reward was placed on his life. When one became too troublesome, the militia was usually called out and the bear quickly destroyed. A grizzly didn't stand much chance against twenty or thirty smoothbore guns. When rewards were offered, most were low and the bears that were hunted down were usually killed by parties of dons who made a holiday event of the affair.

The reata was the Spaniard's favorite tool for recreation and work. They considered it great sport to rout out a huge grizzly and then rope him with sixty-five foot reatas. Many such encounters resulted in the death of some member of the party. Grizzlies that were roped were often taken to the Missions where, in pits or open fields, they were used to stage bear, or bear and bull, fights. Others were just lassoed by the throat and hind legs with a horseman on each end, the two pulling in opposite directions until the grizzly succumbed, generally helped by a knife thrust. Still others were tied down and a sharp horned bull brought to the spot and thrown down. They were fastened together by a rope about thirty feet in length. This was done by tying one end of the rope to a hindleg of the grizzly and the other end to the foreleg of the bull. Then the bull and the bear were allowed to rise. By this time both animals had their "blood up" and were ready to fight. Usually one was killed by the other at the first charge. Sometimes both died of mortal wounds received in the fight that followed, or were finished off by the vaqueros.

Walter Colton's story *Three Years in California* includes the following extract from his diary:

October 28, 1847: The king of all field sports in California is the bear hunt. I determined to witness one, and for this purpose joined a company of native gentlemen bound out on this wild amusement. All were well mounted, armed with rifles and pistols, and provided with reatas. A ride of fifteen miles among mountain crags, which frown in stern wildness over the tranquil beauty of Monterey, brought us to a deserted shanty, in the midst of a gloomy forest of cypress and oak. In a break of this swinging gloom lay a natural pasture, isled in the center by a copse of willows and birch, and on which the sunlight fell. This, it was decided, should be the arena of the sport; a wild bullock was shot, and the quarters, after being trailed around the copse, to scent the bear, were deposited in its shade. The party now retired to the shanty, where our henchmen tumbled from his panniers several rolls of bread, a boiled ham, and a few bottles of London porter. These discussed, and our hourses tethered, each wrapped himself in his blanket, and with his saddle for his pillow, rolled down for repose.

At about twelve o'clock of the night, our watch came into camp and informed us that a bear had just entered the copse. In an instant each sprung to his feet and into the saddle. It was a still, cloudless night, and the moonlight lay in sheets on rivulet, rock and plain. We proceeded with a cautious, noiseless step, through the moist grass of the pasture to the copse in its center, where each took his station, forming a cordon around the little grove. The horse was the first to discover, through the glimmering shade, the stealthful movements of his antagonist. His ears were thrown forward, his nostrils distended, his breathing became heavy and oppressed, and his large eye was fixed immovably on the dim form of the savage animal. Each rider now uncoiled his lasso from its loggerhead, and held it ready to spring from his hand, like a hooped serpent from the break. The bear soon discovered the trap that had been laid for him; plunged from the thicket, broke through the cordon, and was leaping, with giant bounds, over the cleared plot for the dark covert of the forest beyond. A shout arose—a hot pursuit followed and lasso after lasso fell in curving lines around the bear, till at last, one looped him around the neck and brought him to a momentary stand.

As soon as bruin felt the lasso, he growled his defiant thunder, and sprung in rage at the horse. Here came in the sagacity of that noble animal. He knew, as well as his rider, that the safety of both depended on his keeping the lasso taut, and without the admonitions of rein or spur, bounded this way and that, to the front or rear, to accomplish his object, never once taking his eye from the ferocious foe, and ever in the attitude to foil his assaults. The bear, in desperation, seized the lasso in his gripping paws, and hand over hand drew it into his teeth; a moment more and he would have been within leaping distance of his victim; but the horse sprung at the instant, and with a sudden whirl, tripped the bear, and extricated the lasso. At this crowning feat the horse fairly danced with delight. A shout went up which seemed to shake the wildwood with its echoes. The bear plunged again, when the lasso slipped from its loggerhead and bruin was instantly leaping over the field to reach his jungle. The horse, without spur or rein, dashed after him; while his rider, throwing himself over his side, and hanging there like a lamprey eel to a flying sturgeon, recovered his lasso, bruin was brought up again all standing, more frantic and furious than before, while the horse pranced and curveted around him like a savage in his death-dance over his doomed captive. In all this, no overpowering torture was inflicted on old bruin, unless it were through his own rage—which sometimes towers so high he drops dead at your feet. He was now lassoed to a sturdy oak and wound so closely to its body with reata over reata, as to leave him with no scope for breaking or grinding off his clankless chain; though his struggles were often terrific as those of Laocoon, in the resistless folds of the serpent.

This accomplished the company retired again to the shanty, but in spirits too high and noisy for sleep. Day glimmered, and four of the vaqueros started off for a wild bull, which they lassoed out of a roving herd, and in a few hours brought into camp, as full of fury as the bear. Bruin was now cautiously unwound and stood front to front with his horned antagonist. We retreated on our horses to the rim of a large circle, leaving the arena to the two monarchs of the forest and field. Conjectures went wildly around on the issue and the excitement became momently more intense. They stood motionless, as if lost in wonder and indignant astonishment at this strange encounter. Neither turned from the other his blazing eyes; while menace and defiance began to lower in the looks of each. Gathering their full strength the terrific rush was made the bull missed, while the bear, with one enormous bound, dashed his teeth into his back to break the spine. The bull fell, but whirled his huge horn deep into the side of his antagonist. There they lay, grappled and gored, in their convulsive struggles and death throes. We spurred up and with our rifles and pistols closed the tragedy; and it was time; this last scene was too full of blind rage and madness even for the wild sports of a California bear-hunt.

Grizzly Bears of California

OTHER CALIFORNIA GRIZZLIES

No grizzlies have been known to exist in California since 1922. They were thought to have been exterminated within the state by 1915. However, a grizzly bear was shot by Jesse B. Agnew near his cattle ranch at Horse Corral Meadow, Tulare County, California, in August, 1922. Several calves had been lost a short time before. A lower canine tooth was the only part of this animal saved. Dr. C. Hart Merriam examined the tooth and declared it alone was sufficient proof that the bear was a grizzly.

In the 1880's and early 1890's, Henry Miller, of the famed Miller and Lux cattle combine, had a standing bounty of $25 per head for grizzlies killing cattle on his California ranches in the San Joaquin Valley foothills. The same held good on his ranches in Oregon and those along the east slopes of the Sierra Nevada Mountains in Nevada. He paid but few rewards and none were for habitual stock-killing grizzlies.

The late Juan Martinez of Redding, California, an oldtime foreman of one of Miller's San Joaquin ranches, told how he and five other vaqueros roped a female and her cub on one of Miller's ranches in the middle 1880's.

Grizzly roping was practiced by cowmen all over the west. The late Charles M. Russell, Montana's (and America's) greatest cowboy artist, painted several canvases portraying the grizzly. Two of them, entitled "Capturing the Grizzly" and "Ropes and Swift Horses Are Surer Than Lead," show perfect examples of this dangerous sport. Other Russell canvases, such as "Who Killed the Bear," "A Disputed Trail," and "At Close Quarters," verify the true actions of the grizzlies. Charles M. Russell lived in and knew the Old West, and reproduced it on canvas in a truthful, realistic manner.

H. T. Liliencrantz, writer and authority on authentic early

California bear lore, says, "I have a great deal of material on grizzly bears—a very interesting subject—and yet . . . I do not know of a single outstanding outlaw stock-killing grizzly. . . . James C. Adams, a man of the last century, raised a couple of grizzly bears to be both pets and companions. Very few people of today know that grizzlies have been tamed."

The only bear of note to become an outlaw in California after the '49ers arrived was a grizzly known as El Tejon. The bear ranged from mid-summer 1890 to the spring of 1891. Strictly a cattle and horse killer, the bear was roped and shot by three Mexican vaqueros. The reward on his head was $150. Instead of the money, the Mexicans each took a spirited horse in payment.

Several references pertaining to marauding grizzly bears were obtained from old newspapers in the California State Library. A few of the more interesting ones are reprinted here.

Pacific Slope Intelligence, California
SONOMA—*The Democrat* of Sept. 12 says:
Tom Trosper has killed the enormous bear that for many years ravaged the hills and valleys of Salt Point District. Last week, on Austin Creek, Tom met his old enemy and this time proved conqueror. Two year since he encountered this monster grizzly and was left for dead, since then this four-legged "lord of the manor" has destroyed cattle, sheep, etc., it is said, at least $5,000 worth.
—*San Francisco Daily*, Alta, California, Sept. 14, 1868.

San Luis Rey, California
THAT BIG BEAR—A correspondent at San Luis Rey gives us the following particulars of the killing of a formidable bear in that section, noted by us yesterday:
"On Thursday, Oct. 24th, a large bear, weighing over 1,000 pounds, was killed about 25 miles from San Luis Rey by K. Galsh, Wm. Wallace, John Combs, B. F. Libby, and W. B. Couts. The monster was chased for two days, and finally brought to a stop by some favorite dogs belonging to Messrs. Combs and McCarty, when he was shot. This bear has done great damage to the stock raisers for several years past and is supposed to be the same one that Mr. A. E. Maxey offered a big reward for, two years since. *General*, a pet dog of Mr. Combs, deserves creditable mention for the way he behaved in the chase.
—*San Diego Daily Union*, November 2, 1871.

The *Sacramento Bee,* Sacramento, California, in 1950, re-counted the story of Joseph V. Hessig, Siskiyou county's mightiest bear hunter, concerning the identity of a stock-killing grizzly that had been killed in the area in 1890. Hessig has been hunting bears for 58 years, killing four in 1949. At that time, 1950, the ghost of a bear called Clubfoot, killed in 1890 near Hornbrook, had been reportedly seen in London, England, and Paris, France. Hessig stated that the bear under discussion was not Clubfoot but Reelfoot. Clubfoot ranged Butte Valley from the eastern edge of the Cascade Mountains into Modoc County. He had one foot taken off by a trap and was poisoned near the old Dorris Ranch in Butte Valley in the early 1890's.

Hessig claimed that Reelfoot, the grizzly mistakenly called Clubfoot, was a more intelligent animal and ranged from Camp Creek, near Hornbrook, to the eastern edge of the Cascades, never trespassing on the real Clubfoot's territory.

Reelfoot lost two toes in a trap, also several teeth in trying to tear the trap off. He seldom went back to a carcass the second time, which prevented ranchers from poisoning him.

William Wright and Pearl Bean killed Reelfoot in 1890. They had him mounted and exhibited him in a wooden box with the sides let down, for twenty-five cents a look. When the Academy of Science in San Francisco was completed, Reelfoot was sold to it for $250. Hessig, attending school in San Francisco, saw two grizzly bears in the Academy when it opened. He was positive that one of the two was Reelfoot. The Academy and all of its contents burned to the ground in 1906.

The *San Francisco Daily,* published in Alta, California, and dated April 15, 1875, reproduced the following news item:

A BEAR FIGHT

From The Anaheim Gazette

A terrific combat took place on the 5th, between Messrs. W. Carter and Jonathan Watson and a noted bear, known as "White Face," which has long been the scourge and terror of the Santiago Mountains, which resulted in serious, though not fatal injuries to Carter, and the death of his bearship. The gentlemen were travelling through the mountains in search of pasture for their flocks when they suddenly came upon

the huge grizzly which immediately attacked Mr. Carter, knocking
him down before he could draw and cock his pistol. The bear made
two terrible bites at his breast, tearing the flesh in the most horrible
manner, and immediately pursued Mr. Watson, who had retreated in
order to procure time to prepare his rifle for action. Mr. Watson fired
a ball from his Henry rifle, which lodged behind the fore shoulder of
the infuriated brute, but produced no effect except to enrage him
still more. Another shot entered his thick hide without avail. At the
third trial the rifle missed fire from a defective cartridge. When the
bear was within six feet of Mr. Watson, he fired a fourth shot, and
succeeded in sending a ball through the skull just above the eye, which
stretched the monster at his feet. The wounded man was conveyed
to his house, and is now in a fair way of recovering from the injury.
This bear has caused much trouble in the mountains and has destroyed
many sheep belonging to the San Joaquin Company. They will,
doubtless, be pleased to hear of his capture by the Angel of Death.

From the *Petaluma Journal* of June 15th, 1860, the *Sacramento
Daily Union* told of a grizzly in Marin County known as "big
bear of Marin." For four or five years the grizzly had plagued
stock raisers and ranchmen of the region. It was thought that
age and experience had led him to discontinue his early practice
of returning several times to feed upon a kill, since he might find
the remains sprinkled with poison. Numerous attempts were
made to destroy the grizzly, but to no avail. At one time he was
lassoed by a party of native Californians who came upon him
in an opening. The grizzly planted himself on his haunches,
seized the lariat and commenced gathering it in, each haul bringing the horse and rider nearer until the rope was cut and the
attempt at capture abandoned.

On the 7th of June, 1869, the grizzly invaded the premises of
J. S. Bracket, near Salmon Creek, and feasted on a hog. The
following day, Brackett led a group of men in following the bear's
trail. They had gone but a short distance into a wood when the
bear appeared without warning. Bonnard, a member of the
party, fired without effect as the bear made for him and "crushed
him to the earth." Another member of the party shot the grizzly
in the neck, killing him. Bonnard suffered only a slight flesh
wound on the left arm. The grizzly weighed 1,140 pounds.

The popularity of the grizzly bear in California in 1856 is

evident in the paragraphs from "A Condensation of the Introduction" to *The Adventures of James Capen Adams, Mountaineer and Grizzly Bear Hunter of California,* by Theodore H. Hittell.

In the early part of October, 1856, while in charge of the local department of the Daily Evening Bulletin newspaper of San Francisco, my attention was attracted to a small placard on a basement door on Clay, near Leidesdorff street. It announced the exhibition there of "The Mountain Museum," a collection of wild animals of the Pacific Coast, the principal of which were "Samson, the largest grizzly bear ever caught, weighing over 1500 pounds, Lady Washington (with her cub) weighing 1000 pounds, and Benjamin Franklin, King of the Forest."

Descending the stairway, I found a remarkable spectacle. The basement was large but with a low ceiling, and dark and dingy in appearance. In the middle, chained to the floor, were two large grizzly bears, which proved to be Lady Washington and Benjamin Franklin. They were pacing restlessly in circles some 10 feet in dameter, occasionally rearing up, and reversing their direction. Not far off on one side, likewise on chains, were 7 other bears, several of them young grizzlies, three or four black bears, and one cinnamon. Near the front was an open stall, in which were haltered two large elks. Further back were cages, containing cougars and other California animals; a few eagles and other birds. At the rear, in a very large iron cage, was the monster grizzly Samson, immense, weighing ¾ ton. From his looks and actions, as well as from the care taken to rail him off from spectators, it was evident that he was not to be approached too closely.

In the midst of this strange menagerie was Adams, the proprietor— quite as strange as any of his animals. He was a little over medium size, muscular and wiry, sharp features and penetrating eyes; about fifty years of age, hair very gray, beard very white. He was dressed in coat and pantaloons of buckskin, fringed at edges and along seams of arms and legs. A cap of deerskin, ornamented with a foxtail, on his feet buckskin moccasins.

I became particularly interested in the bears Ben Franklin and Lady Washington. Adams seemed to have perfect control over them; he placed his hand on their jaws, and even in their mouths, to show their teeth, made them rear on hind legs and walk erect, growl when he ordered them to talk, and perform various tricks. He put them to boxing and wrestling, sometimes with himself, sometimes with each other; they went through all performances with good nature, and great apparent enjoyment of the sport.

I noticed that hair was worn off portions of their backs. Adams said it was caused by pack saddles. He gave a brief account of how he had lived in the mountains for several years; how he had caught and trained his bears, and how on occasions he had used them as pack animals. He loosed Ben Franklin, and jumping on his back, rode several times around the apartment. He next threw a bag of grain upon the animal's back and the bear carried it as if used to the task.

After showing a month or two, Adams hired and fitted up the spacious first floor of the California Exchange on the corner of Kearny and Clay streets, where in December, 1856, he established the "Pacific Museum." There until August, 1859, thereafter in the Pavilion Building on the site of the present Lick House until the end of 1859, he continued to give exhibitions, which were witnessed by many thousands of visitors.

During those years Adams lived among his animals; he continued to wear buckskin. Between July 1857 and December, 1859, he narrated to me his adventures in full, understanding my purpose to be, if story sufficiently interesting, to make a book.

An edition was published at Boston, and also at San Francisco in 1860, just before the breaking out of the Civil War; but on account of various troubles, mostly occasioned by the war, went out of print. Present new edition (1911) is same form and material as first.

Adams moved to New York, sailing on Clipper ship "Golden Fleece," January 7, 1860; voyage 3½ months. He there made a contract with Phineas T. Barnum and thenceforth exhibited in connection with Barnum's Shows.

He died a year later, from complications caused by injuries received in earlier life, at Neponset, near Boston, where relatives resided.

—Theodore H. Hittell, 1926.

Grizzly Bears of Alaska

In Alaska, the grizzly bear is far from extinct. Their behavior and habits in the Alaska country, due to climatic and food conditions, are much different from those of grizzlies found in the other western states. Since I have studied the Alaskan grizzly but little, I do not feel competent to comment on them. However, two grizzly incidents that happened in Alaska are worth telling here.

Tobogganing

I have seen many bear toboggan slides, but Ed Francis, aged trapper and prospector of Alaska's Tanana River country, was the first to tell me of seeing a bear in the act of tobogganing.

In the spring of 1910, Ed was coming up a twisting trail that skirted the north end of a ridge. A stand of timber was above the trail, but below it a gradual open slope, snow-covered to a depth of about two feet, angled downward for almost a hundred feet. At the foot of the slope was a snow-packed gully.

A sharp turn on the trail revealed a grizzly on the trail up ahead of him. Ed ducked behind some boulders, sat down, and watched. The bear was approximately one hundred fifty feet away. He was about two years old, gaunt, and probably hadn't been out of hibernation long. He was the first one Ed had seen that spring. The wind was blowing from the bear to Ed. The bear was standing with his back to Ed, looking down the slope below the trail.

All at once the bear stepped off the trail, sat down at the top of the slope, raised his hind paws a little, leaned somewhat forward, wiggled his body, and suddenly went shooting downward amid a flurry of fine snow.

He hit the snow bank at the bottom and went end over middle.

When he stopped rolling, he righted and shook himself, and looked up the slope, with a satisfied expression on his face. Then he started down the gully, stopped abruptly, and looked back at the trail he had made on the slope in sliding down.

Like a child with a new sled, he turned about and started up the slope in the path of his slide. At the top he sat down on his haunches and looked down at his tracks in the snow. His tongue was lolled out a little and he was obviously tickled. He moved to the crest of the slope, as he had done before, sat down, gave a wiggle with his body to get started, and down he went a-flying. When he got straightened out at the bottom, he looked up the slope as happy as could be. Then he moved down the gully. A few moments later, Ed heard a mad crashing of brush. Evidently, the bear had scented him and was on his way to safer places.

Lost Dinner

A sudden meeting of wild game and a grizzly was told to my father by Tom Shea, an Alaskan sourdough who saw an aged grizzly unexpectedly come upon a band of bighorn sheep. The year was 1901. High in Alaska's Wrangel Mountains Shea was on a bench looking down on another bench across a crevice. The crevice was about twenty feet wide and approximately a hundred feet deep. Both walls were very steep with small rocky juts sticking out from them.

The bench across from Tom had a half-circle, high rock bank at the back with a low depression in the center of it. Suddenly through the depression two rams, three ewes, and two kids bounded onto the bench. Being well concealed, he watched, careful to be still and quiet. The kids were about three months old. They started playing immediately while the other sheep began to feed. Like children playing follow-the-leader, the kids jumped from one boulder to another, landing with perfect balance. Sometimes they would run straight at their mothers, then jump clear over them. They were quick, graceful, and sure-footed. Their play was interrupted when the older sheep abruptly spun about and faced the rock bank as a big, brownish-furred grizzly came through the depression onto the bench. With the wind blowing the way it was, the meeting was a sudden surprise to both the bear and the sheep. The bear stood up on its hind legs and looked at the sheep. It appeared that the grizzly thought it had the bighorns cornered.

The two rams were about thirty feet apart and a little farther than that from the bear. After a few seconds pause, one ram took a step toward the grizzly. The other ram lowered his head a little. Both stood tense. The ewes and kids had dashed to a point on the bench at the edge of the crevice. From a flat stand, a ewe seemingly leaped downward into space. She landed on a jut of rock on Tom's side of the crevice wall. From there she leaped downward to a rocky point on the other wall. After a slight pause, she again leaped downward to a small ledge-like protrusion on the other wall, and from it to the dry creek bottom that formed the floor of the crevice. About the time she left the first jut, a kid leaped from the bench and followed her descent. The kid was quickly followed by another ewe, the other kid, and the last ewe. At one time two ewes and a kid were leaping one way or the other across the crevice at the same time. It was a great thing to see, and held his interest so that he forgot momentarily about the grizzly and the rams.

When he remembered to look at them, the bear had dropped to all fours and was about to rush one of the rams. Just as it started, the rams broke and dashed toward and past each other like a streak of lightning. Their action confused the grizzly and it paused. That pause gave both rams time to turn sharply and, one behind the other, race to the edge of the bench. They swiftly leaped downward in the same pattern the ewes and kids had followed. The grizzly reached the edge of the bench just as the last ram landed on a jut across the crevice. The bear paced along the shoulder of the bench in vexation and rage, watching the rams as they leaped downward and away from danger. In agitation the bear watched until they all disappeared, then in a disgusted manner, he lumbered off through the depression.

Grizzly Bears of British Columbia

At Mill Bay, located at the mouth of the Nass River in northern British Columbia, I met Dutch Banister. He had spent fifty-one years as a guide, packer, prospector, and trapper throughout British Columbia, Alberta, Northwestern Territory, Canada, and various parts of Alaska. He was still going strong at seventy-four, with more energy than any man of his age I have ever met. With him, I had the opportunity to observe and study the actions of more grizzlies than I had ever encountered in the western United States.

We worked together eight months. Between pack trips, we made one hunting trek after mountain sheep, mountain goats, and moose, in addition to spending all available spare time watching grizzlies.

Fish are the food the grizzly likes best. From June to October various species of salmon (humpback, silver, sockeye) run up the Alaskan and Canadian rivers, and the bears are on hand to greet them. The grizzly knows when fishing season starts in his territory and never gets mixed up on his dates. About ten days before the salmon run begins in his locality, the grizzly leaves the high country and works his way down to the lower streams and rivers. The grizzly selects a shallow riffle, near cover, where he can lie up when not fishing.

W. H. Wright, veteran grizzly hunter of years gone by, who has hunted the great bears all over the northwestern United States and in the Selkirk Mountains in Canada, tells of watching their fishing methods in both riffles and pools.

"The grizzly," Wright relates, "usually sits on the bank of the stream and watches the riffles over which the salmom try to force their way. He will wait quietly enough until the salmon is about halfway up the riffle and struggling in its efforts to make the ascent. Then he will make a quick dash and, with one sweep of his huge paw, will send a shower of water ten feet into the air, in the midst of which will be seen a salmon sailing toward the creek bank and landing, many times, ten to twenty feet beyond. Then the bear hurriedly makes for the shore, and if hungry, eats the fish. If he has already had his fill, he will kill it, lay it down and, returning, wait for another. I have seen one bear catch seventeen salmon in this manner before stopping; and he then carefully piled them together and buried them for future use.

"Sometimes a bear will sit on a log penetrating into the water and watch for fish to swim out from under the log. When one comes, he will, with a sweep of his paw, send it flying to the bank. I have often seen them fishing in this way, lying on a log with one paw hanging in the water. It is wonderful how many salmon they will fling out."

The grizzlies in the Nass River district come down from the high country soon after hibernation to fish in the river and its tributary streams when the spring salmon runs start. They stay until early fall. During that time millions of salmon, fighting their way upstream to spawn and die, offer a continuous feast to grizzlies and the bear family in general.

The grizzly's fishing procedure in that area was simple and direct. They waded into shallow riffles and, when a run of salmon came by, either grabbed one in the mouth or pinned it to the stream-bed with a fore paw and picked it up in the mouth. They then carried it onto the bank and ate what they wanted of it, or buried it for future use.

In a shallow stream, on two occasions, we saw one big fellow hook a salmon on its tine-like claws. Whether the claw catching maneuver was accidental or intentional, I do not know. The salmon became spiked on the claws after the bear began a cup-like, upward sweep with his paw, similar to the movement used in batting fish onto the bank. Both times the bear quickly grabbed the fish in its mouth and carried it out onto the bank to eat it.

We watched a big, dark-gray grizzly, with frosty tipped fur on his massive shoulders, pin a salmon with his paw. He then took it in his mouth, and as he started for the bank, he suddenly pinned another. Remaining motionless for a few moments in indecision, he watched the salmon under his paw, the thrashing tail splashing water into his face. Then he nosed down in an attempt to get it between his teeth. In doing so, the one in his mouth got away. As he made a frantic lunge to recover the escapee, the one under his paw got away. The bear then turned completely around in "I'll be—" fashion, and shortly caught another which he carried out on the bank and ate. Returning to the creek, he stood on the bank for some time, watching salmon break water as they fought their way over the riffles. After a while he entered the water again where we left him fishing peacefully.

The best way to stalk bears along a water course is to wade in the water. Foot scent is destroyed by so doing. If one walked on land, the scent would be left for many hours.

One place from which we watched is vividly remembered because of its scenic beauty and the number of adult grizzlies we saw there. We approached the spot by wading up a creek to a sharp bend. The banks were heavily timbered and the trees, which came down to the water's edge, gave the impression of wading in a canyon. A fallen tree lay across the creek at the bend. Its middle, broken by the fall, was partly submerged in the water. We climbed upon the bank and concealed ourselves in a dense growth of prickly devil's club near the trunk of the fallen tree. From our position we could see both sides of the upstream for about sixty yards. In that space the stream widened out as it passed through a small clearing. Heavy timber and a dense cover of ferns and devil's club lined most of the gravel banks that flanked the sides of the creek. The creek was about twenty-five feet wide and for the whole sixty yards flowed swiftly over shallow riffles.

No bears were in sight when we took our stand, but fresh remains of salmon on the banks indicated bears had been there recently. Before long a large, blackish-brown grizzly emerged from a trail in the heavy ferns, crossed the bank, splashed into the creek, and immediately began fishing. Soon a medium-sized, dark-grayish grizzly appeared across the creek and almost opposite the first one. He approached the creek a few yards below the other bear and began to fish. A little later, splashing down the center of the creek at the head of the riffle, another grayish-

177

brown fellow appeared. After advancing some distance, he, too, began to fish. None of them paid any attention to the others, although they were within fifty feet of each other most of the time. When they departed, each went his own way.

We returned to the same place a few days later. It was mid-morning, clear and sunny. When we took our stand in the ferns, a young grizzly was fishing in the middle of the riffle about thirty yards away. We always hunted up-wind, but while we watched a cross-current of air must have carried our scent to the bear, for suddenly he stood up and looked our way. In our hidden position we knew he could not see us. He was a typical gray silver-tip and made a beautiful picture standing in the bright sunlight with the white-flecked water racing past him. After a time, he turned about, dropped on all fours, and continued fishing; but he was nervous and soon left by way of the ferns and timber above the riffles.

Knowing of the grizzly's inquisitive nature, I decided to try something I had long wanted to do. I waded up-stream about fifteen yards to a log with a skyward pointing limb. The log lay parallel to the creek's course beside one bank. There I dipped a small, white rag into the water, tied it to the limb and returned to our fern hideout. The rag soon dried and began to flop in the breeze.

Before long, a large grizzly, still with patches of his winter coat upon him, made his appearance on a bank and advanced to the creek. After catching a salmon, he continued across the creek to the opposite bank. The wind was blowing from the bear to the rag. It was about fifty feet from the bear. The grizzly was lowering his head to take a bite out of the salmon when he noticed the white, fluttering object. For a moment he paused, again started to lower his head, then jerked it up as his ears came forward. Standing motionless and intent for a few seconds, he eyed the rag. Disregarding the salmon, he suddenly took a few steps forward. Next he made a half-circular advance as he walked into the creek. A few feet from the rag, he stopped and stood up. Seconds passed. Then he ambled forward on his hind legs and stuck his nose close to it. Regardless of having been dipped in water, some human scent must have remained on the cloth. With a loud woof, he made a turning jump, landed on all fours with a mighty splash, crossed the creek, and walked briskly toward the timber. Near its edge, he stopped, half-turned as he looked back, then made a hasty exit into the ferns at the timber's edge.

While with Dutch, we came upon two grizzly rubbing posts. One was a tree sheared off by lightning about twenty feet above the ground. The other was a tall, dead tree. Around the base of both posts masses of bear fur were caught in the bark where the bears had scratched themselves. Chunks of bark had been either bitten or torn off to a height of twelve feet above the ground. It is commonly and erroneously believed that a rubbing post is used by a bear ranging in the territory to warn others to keep out of its domain. Rubbing posts are used by bears to scratch themselves, as well as to let other bears know of their prowess and proximity. Several grizzlies and black and brown bears may use the same post.

Tom Lloyd, prospector and hunter, told me about a humorous rubbing post scene that happened in British Columbia's Frazier River country. He was on a knoll looking down on a small clearing in the timber about forty yards away. On the far side was a rubbing post, a burned stump of a tree nearly thirty feet high. About three feet in front of it was the stump of a smaller tree which had broken off about fourteen feet above the ground. In falling, the butt of the broken tree had wedged itself between the post and its own stump. The rest of the tree sloped backward to the ground.

Just as Tom was leaving, a large, black bear came into the clearing and up to the post. After scratching himself, he stood up, stretched his forelegs above his head, and clawed the bark. He stopped quickly, threw his head back and looked upward. Until then, Tom had not noticed a freshly clawed grizzly spot on the post. It was four and one-half feet above the black bear's mark, which was seven feet above ground. Right away the black bear began sniffing around. Soon he backed off a few feet, sat down, and moved his head up and down as he looked at the grizzly's mark and then at his own. The grizzly's mark must have displeased him and caused some disbelief, for he went back to the post, stretched up as high as he could and clawed again. Then he circled the post twice, all the time looking upward. After the third circle, he disappeared.

Seconds later came the sound of cracking brush. Then he came walking up the fallen tree. Upon reaching the butt, which was stuck between the post and the tree stump, he stretched out on his belly, hugged the tree with all fours, swung his neck and head over, and sniffed the grizzly's mark. Releasing his hold on the tree with one paw, he stretched the paw out and touched the grizzly's mark ever so lightly. After another sniff or two, he was evidently satisfied that there was a bigger bear in the woods than he was. He went back down the tree and disappeared into the timber.

Black and brown bears are considered the clowns of the woods and the scavengers of the forest, but that was one of the darndest things Lloyd said he had ever seen any bear do.

One day while Dutch Banister and I were bathing in a creek, I noticed the upper back part of his left shoulder and arm bore deep scars. It was hard to get Dutch to talk about himself, but finally he told me how they came to be there.

In late summer in the foothills of British Columbia's Peak Mountains, he was coming down a heavily timbered slope. At its base was a grassy clearing with a dense clump of blue currant in a little pocket-like indentation at the foot of the hill. He came out of the woods at one end of the currant clump. As he started around it, to cross the clearing, he heard a sudden woofing-growl and a crashing of brush close behind him. Ducking low, he spun around just in time to catch a grizzly's claw across his shoulder and upper arm. The blow knocked his rifle out of his hand and knocked him to the ground. Dazed, he lay there a moment or two. He knew it was always best to lie still when downed by a grizzly, or any bear, but being dazed, he made the mistake of trying to get up. The bear grabbed his left arm in its mouth, drew blood, and shook him. When it let go, Dutch landed sideways and lay still. He couldn't see the bear because it was behind him, but he could hear it moving around close by, all the time woofing low. In a little while, it moved off into the timber.

Dutch made a tourniquet at his shoulder and stopped the

bleeding from his arm. The grizzly hadn't bitten deep. It was more of a pinch, but when shaking him it tore the flesh badly. He had a small pack on his back which took most of the wallop, so he didn't get clawed so deeply there. Dutch found his rifle on top of the currant bushes, ten feet away. The bear probably had been sleeping in the bushes and, when startled at close quarters, had charged. Dutch made his way to his cabin and his mining partner took him to town and to the doctor.

In twenty-seven years, Dutch knew of only four men being attacked and mauled by grizzlies. I have met only two, Dutch being one. Fortunately, all the men attacked were "bear wise" and when knocked down lay still until the grizzly had departed. In all cases, the bears were either come upon suddenly at close quarters, or wounded. When the grizzlies charged, they came with direct, wild, rushing bounds on all fours. None ever stood up after the charge began, or hugged their victims, as so often described and pictured. They bit, clawed, and mauled; then as quickly as the attack began, they stopped, and soon retreated to the nearest cover.

In all Dutch's years in grizzly country, he said he had seen only one absolutely unprovoked charge by a grizzly. He was hunting mountain sheep in Northwestern Territory of Canada and had just downed a ram when the grizzly came over the crest of a barren, rocky ridge about seventy-five yards away. It charged down the slope at an angle toward him. He fired two 30-06 slugs into the bear and it dropped fifteen yards from him.

Grizzlies rarely cover their kills. The last day Dutch and I spent observing bears, we came upon the remains of a doe buried by a grizzly under a pile of dirt and debris. It was evident that the bear had returned once after covering it. We followed its tracks to a place nearby where the bear had rested between meals. It was a slight rise about one hundred feet from the doe, in a position from which the bear could see the cache. Only the doe's head, neck and part of one shoulder remained. They were so badly torn it was impossible to determine if the bear had killed it, or if some other animal had been the killer and the bear happened upon it afterwards. However, grizzlies of the Alaska, British Columbia, and Northwestern Territory coun-

181

try occasionally kill deer, mountain sheep, and goats, and sometimes have been known to kill caribou and moose. Since there were no visible signs or tracks of other animals about, we felt safe in assuming the does remains were the result of the grizzly's work.

I once used a 30-30 on grizzlies. At the time Dutch and I were on a pack job in northern British Columbia, transporting explosives to a mine high on a mountain side. We had twelve mules in our string, each loaded with four boxes of dynamite, two boxes in each bag. Handling explosives is dangerous anytime, but especially so with unpredictable mules in an unnerving situation.

We had stopped the mules to rest them before starting up a long, loose-rock ridge. While resting we noticed a she-grizzly and her two yearling cubs ambling about near the crest of the ridge we were to ascend. When they disappeared over the ridge, we calculated they would go down the other side into the timber, which we knew was there. We quickly forgot about them as we started up the trail.

At the top of the ridge was a small, boulder-strewn saddle which sloped gradually downward to timber. The lead mule, Lop Ears by name, was almost in the center of the saddle when he suddenly let go a startled bray and sat back on his hind legs. Instantly the other mules stopped in their tracks, ridgedly alert. I was ahead of Dutch and when my saddle horse stopped, I saw his ears prick forward. I drew my 30-30 from the scabbard and dismounted. By that time my horse's nostrils were dilating as he tested the wind with sharp bursts of air.

Lop Ears and the two mules directly behind him brayed excitedly and turned from the trail. Two went one way, and Lop Ears the other, toward timber.

My horse had stopped among several, huge, flattopped boulders. The boulders and the mules before me hindered my sight of the trail ahead. To gain a better view, I scrambled up on one of the boulders, as did Dutch on another across from me. When I stood up, the she-grizzly and her two cubs were charging toward the mules which were scattering in all directions. Lop Ears, with two other mules close behind him, was headed straight for the timber with the intention, I believe, of raking off their

182

packs by going between trees growing close together. The bears were coming full speed and were less than forty yards away, and the she-bear, having forgotten about the mules, had centered her attention on my horse.

Suddenly I heard Dutch yell, "Jump for cover!" As I did so, there was an almighty roar. I landed beside my horse just as he pinwheeled on his hind legs, his body knocking me to the ground between two boulders. I landed on my stomach, but somehow held on to my rifle.

The next instant there came another explosion, as the shower of gravel from the first one began descending from the heavens. I covered my head with my hands and crowded close to the base of one of the boulders. By that time stones were flying and bouncing all around me.

Moments later I saw one of the cubs dash by, turn suddenly, and dive between two boulders. He was less than twenty feet away and in plain view. There came another tremendous roar. This was followed by more flying stones as the cub turned completely around, dropped flat on his belly, rolled himself into a ball, and with his nose between his forefeet, never moved until the commotion was over. While gravel was still descending, I did some fast thinking. As soon as it stopped, I jumped up. Dust, kicked up by the explosions, was heavy in the air.

Up the trail I could barely see the mother bear as she gained her feet. It was obvious she had been injured or stunned by flying rocks. She began to bawl wrathfully. Seconds later the other cub ran up to her. She knocked him out of her way and dashed toward me. I raised the 30-30 and fired three times. It later developed that two of the bullets hit her in the back and shoulder. The other bullet struck her in the head. When she went down, she never moved again.

The cub in the rocks suddenly let go a woof. Turning, I saw him standing on his hind legs, eyeing me. I fired from hip level due to boulder obstructions. The bullet struck him in the side and he fell over. Moving position, I fired again at the base of his skull as he started to rise. He quivered a moment and relaxed. Quickly I jammed two cartridges into the carbine and turned my attention to the other cub. He was running toward a shaking mule. I fired twice and he went down, rolled over, regained his feet, ran a few yards and dropped dead.

The air was still hazy with dust when Dutch appeared from behind the boulder from which he had jumped. During the whole affair he had not been in a shooting position. When he had jumped he had landed on a slope of small, loose rocks, and slid down it several yards into a hollow.

We took stock of the mess and found four mules missing. The last explosion must have been a double one and accounted for the fourth mule. We never found any part of the missing four. Some of the others were cut up by flying rocks. Why the packs on the others hadn't gone off from the concussion of the explosions is a mystery.

This was my most exciting hunting experience. It is the closest I ever came to going somewhere without getting there.

An old trapper and prospector of British Columbia's Selkirk Mountains recounted to me his eye-witness story about the sudden meeting of a grizzly and mountain goat on a ledge trail. The Selkirks are very steep. The old gentleman was near a cliff edge watching a big grizzly across the canyon from him. The bear was working up a narrow, high ledge trail toward the summit. Just as it reached a sharp turn, two mountain goats, in single file, suddenly appeared coming down the trail. When they met, the bear and the lead goat were less than two yards apart. Both paused for a split second. There was no space for either of the animals to turn about. Without warning the lead goat lunged forward as it lowered its head. With the movement, the bear half reared on its hind feet. On the narrow trail it was probably a difficult feat for the bear and before it could slap out with a paw, the goat hooked him in the chest with his dagger-like horns. The force of the impact knocked the grizzly sideways and it fell off the ledge to its death on the jagged rocks below.

Numerous, reliable accounts tell of grizzlies having slain caribou in both Alaska and Canada, and of caribou having turned and fought off an antagonistic grizzly. When there are young in the herd, caribou will sometimes form a circle around their offspring to defend them, as cattle do, but usually they turn and run from approaching danger.

Irregular Incidents

From time to time, after 1915, newspaper items mentioned a grizzly going on a rampage. These were not habitual stock killers nor in any sense of the word could be considered outlaws. Their escapades, as recorded in the papers, were spread over several years, and varied from the killing of an isolated animal to a single raid on a sheep corral. Compared to an outlaw grizzly, these losses were inconsequential.

In 1927, a grizzly drifted out of Yellowstone Park and for several days ran amuck in the vicinity of Jackson Hole, Wyoming. Snow was on the ground. The bear was undoubtedly on his way to den-up for the winter in the jagged peaks of the Teton Mountains when it met and killed two steers in the foothills. Farther up the mountains it chanced to encounter three bands of elk, bound from their high-meadow summer range for the valley at Jackson Hole, where the U. S. Fish and Wildlife Service feed around 15,000 elk each winter. The grizzly killed a bull and two cows in the first band it came upon. In the second band it killed a yearling bull, and in the third, a cow and two yearlings. Tracks revealed how the grizzly had attacked the elk while they were fighting their way through snow drifts, which prevented their running to safety. The bear was never known to repeat the procedure. It seemed to be one of those things that happen occasionally when domesticated and wild animals meet at close quarters.

Similar incidents in which grizzlies have killed lone elk and deer have been recorded off and on for years, in and near both Glacier and Yellowstone National Parks.

In 1929, an old, grayish-white fellow that had been somewhat of a problem to the Yellowstone Park rangers suddenly became tired of the park's routine way of living and took off to seek adventure in new fields. From the park his route led west around the north end of the Big Bent Ridge in Idaho and into the Rolling

Plains grazing lands. In the twenty-three days before rangers succeeded in eliminating him, he destroyed several ranch dogs, ten head of cattle (some were family milk cows), invaded a sheep corral and killed several head, killed two horses and crippled three others at another meeting in a corral.

The bear capped his spree by getting into a rancher's hog pen. There it encountered the wrath of a cantankerous and well-tusked boar. The boar gashed him so severely in their fight that rangers, summoned from the Park after his first escapade and waiting in the vicinity, had no trouble in tracking him down.

Another grizzly, in 1930, invaded a section of the Boulder River Valley, Montana. He killed one hundred-fifty sheep. A government hunter was sent for and the bear was destroyed.

The latest report I have of a grizzly killing livestock comes from Choteau, Montana, in the fall of 1952. The bear invaded the outlying area of the town and killed 32 sheep in a week. He killed six bucks during one night.

Romy McCallum, U. S. government trapper, failed to capture the bear with traps or decoys.

When local men went after him at night, with the aid of two sheep put out as decoys, the grizzly killed the sheep when rain forced the hunters to seek shelter.

After that the bear's tracks led into the mountains. No more depredations followed after his departure from the area.

There is no doubt that grizzlies, being both carnivorous and carrion eaters, when hungry have slain colts, sheep, calves, deer, fawns, and sometimes larger, full grown animals, if they happened upon them. But such killings are few and far between, and the slayers do not wilfully continue the procedure as did the outlaw grizzlies.

An unusual incident occurred in October, 1881, when a grizzly caused the wreck of a stagecoach, simply by crossing the road. The stagecoach driver, James McCabe, wrote of it in a letter to his sister. A guard named Edwards was with him on the driver's seat. A honky-tonk girl, a gambler, and a Chinaman were in the coach as passengers. They were on their way to Virginia City, Montana. His account of the event follows:

186

We was nearing Virginia City. The road followed a ridge running along the edge of a valley. We was going right smartly. I weren't expecting trouble. When we rounded a sharp turn where the road starts down a hill, the leaders suddenly snorted in alarm, bolted and turned off the road at a sharp angle. I drew back on the reins and played on the brake. It didn't do no good. The wheelers turned too, just as sharp and quick. Them horses knowed what they was doing. Up ahead I got a glimpse of a grizzly. The bear was about a hundred yards off. When the wheelers turned, the stage buckled at the sharp angle and went over sideways, throwing me and Ed clear. We landed on the road. I got the wind knocked out of me. I came to at the report of Ed's rifle, and looked up to see him standing over me. The bear got away. The horses were all down, kicking, tangled in their harness, and squealing from fright or pain. The Chinaman was sprawled half in and half out of the coach door on the top side—yelling to beat h—. The gambler had a broken arm and was cussing plenty. The gal got scratched and shook up pretty much. She didn't like it very well. One horse had a broken leg. All of them was bruised up. A front wheel was smashed. Outside of that nobody was hurt much. I sent Ed on a horse to Virginia City for help. It looked like half the population came back with him. They call me "Grizzly" McCabe around here now.

An Excerpt from

ROCKY MOUNTAIN WILDLIFE

by W. M. Rush

I recall a quartet of grizzlies that went on a rampage that took them over a wide territory and resulted in wanton destruction of property, as well as the loss of a lot of winter food supplies.

They began their depredations at Silver Tip Ranch, just north of Yellowstone Park. A garage and storehouse belonging to the ranch stand at the end of automobile travel on lower Slough Creek, three miles from the main highway. The bears may have visited the place several times before the mischief they had done was discovered, as the storehouse was used little during the fall and winter. That I don't know, but it was mid-October when they made their last visit, tore some boards off the oat bin and helped themselves to all the oats they wanted. They wasted more than they ate by scattering it on the ground. They had gained admittance to the building by smashing a window.

About four miles away to the north and over a low, rough hill was Lower Slough Creek Ranger Cabin. It was a small, two-room cabin made out of logs with a board roof covered with tar paper. A one-room cabin nearby was used as a storeroom. It, too, was of logs with a tar paper roof. The windows were protected by heavy plank shutters, the doors stoutly barricaded. Although the roof was not very strong, it was stout enough to keep out rain and snow and no one doubted that was sufficient. The four grizzlies proved otherwise when they climbed upon the roof, tore off some boards, crawled inside, and literally wrecked the place.

The grub box was a heavy one, covered with tin to keep out mice and other rodents and so big it could hardly go through the door. It stood in a corner of the cabin and held dried fruit, a sack of sugar, flour, graham crackers, potatoes, and other staples. The bears broke down the door from the inside, rolled the box out into the yard, and did their best to break it open, without success.

They got little to eat in the cabin. A cupboard on the wall, which contained some sugar and syrup, was pulled from its fastenings and the contents scattered. There was a little ham and bacon in the storehouse. They tore some boards off the roof and went inside the building, tearing down the screened cooler from the wall and eating the meat scraps.

The ranger returned to the scene a few days later. It would be hard to imagine more complete devastation. The roofs were torn off both cabins. Tables, chairs, and stove were upset and broken, the battered grub box was a hundred yards from the house, and the storeroom was a wreck. It was a sizable loss to the ranger. It meant a lot of extra repair work, new things to buy, and a mess to clean up. No wonder he was boiling with indignation and swearing vengeance on the vandals.

His troubles were a mere bagatelle, however, compared to those of Bob LaCombe, keeper of buffaloes, whose headquarters were southeast about eight miles over a high mountain. Bob and his wife, Nora, were away on their vacation somewhere in southern California. His place wasn't unguarded by any means. About sixty yards away was the bunkhouse where Tom Phillips, assistant buffalo keeper, and another man were batching.

Bob had put everything in order before he went away. Potatoes and other perishables were in the cellar under the house where they would not freeze. Water was shut off and all pipes drained. On the dining table, safe from mice, were piled several hundred-pound sacks of sugar, half a dozen sacks of flour, hams and bacon, packages of dried fruit, and various other articles of food, including a five-gallon container of syrup. Bob had laid in a large part of his winter provisions before the roads were snowed up and impassable. In the cupboards were a few jars of home-made jam, some cans partly full of honey and syrup, sugar bowls half full, small cans of spices, salt and pepper. Nora was a wonderful housekeeper. Everything was always spic and span.

That was the setting when the four bears first visited the ranch. There were an old grizzly she-bear and three two-year olds. They arrived on an evening in late October, rather early, right after darkness fell. The two dogs gave them a warm reception, which was seconded by a few shots fired by the men. The bears ran away and no more trouble was anticipated. Next day the men rigged up an elaborate "burglar alarm" just in case the bears decided to come back. Strings and wires were stretched all around the yard and connected with a huge dinner bell that could be heard for two miles when it rang. Tests showed that the alarm system worked perfectly.

Imagine how Tom and his helper felt next morning when they discovered that the marauders had been back, evaded every wire and string, sneaked by the dogs, got inside the house and out again without even disturbing the slumbers of either dogs or men. And the inside of Bob's and Nora's house was a sight!

The bears broke through a "lazy window" into the dining room and cut their feet pretty badly on the shattered window glass. Once inside they proceeded to make a mess. They scattered flour and sugar all over the house, got the syrup can open and let its contents run over the floor. They tore into cupboards, broke glass in them, and even put their bloody, dirty feet on Nora's clean bedspread.

Along with their fun, they had a feast. Whole hams, sides of bacon, sacks of sugar, packages of dried fruits, all the things that bears like to eat were there and everything in generous quantities. What a night for the bruins! Along toward morning they went out through the window and straight across the valley toward Specimen Ridge, leaving a floury, bloody and sugary trail. They headed for the high hills and safety with thoughts which may have run something like this:

"Complete night of it—trail left, of course, but who cares? We got away with it. Bob will be mad. He'll forget all about it by spring. Tom is mad already. We're wise to strings and wires. We have to

189

be if we're to get by, with all the set-guns, traps, and pitfalls there are in this world. A string stretched across the trail might as well be a two-foot log when it comes to us noticing it. We bears are expert observers. We have to be, to live!"

That should have been a fitting climax to their career of crime, but unfortunately it wasn't. A few days later the same four came off Specimen Ridge down to Lamar River about fifteen miles upstream from Buffalo Ranch. A pack train of horses and mules had just been along the trail that extended from the highway at Soda Butte up Lamar River, past Miller Creek Snowshoe Cabin to Cold Creek Cabin and on to Pelican Creek and the main highway near Yellowstone Lake. The pack train was distributing supplies and food to the cabins for winter use of snowshoe travelers who could not carry provisions with them.

The cabin at Miller Creek was an old one, built in early days when there were no funds allotted to buy building materials. It was constructed of stones and logs. Stones made the foundations and fireplace, logs the wall, hewn logs the floors. For the roof more logs were hewn into troughs, the first layer being placed with the hewn side up, the next with the hewn side down, so that they fitted into each other and made a very effective roof to turn water. Covered with a layer of dirt about a foot thick this made a warm shelter, not as clean as might be desired, but the best that could be had without packing in lumber, shingles, and other ready made material from outside.

The packers camped all night in this cabin. Before leaving they saw to it that there was ample bedding hung in a safe place away from rodents, a liberal supply of wood cut, and even shavings and fine sticks for kindling. They put potatoes, canned goods and vegetables into the hole under the floor. Flour, crackers, dried fruit, ham and bacon went into a rodent proof grub box. A sack of oats was hung from the ceiling on a wire, in case one more horse patrol came through the country that fall. When everything was in order, they locked the door and proceeded on their way to the next cabin.

The bears followed the horse tracks and came to the cabin a day or so after the packers left. It had been several days since their feast at Buffalo Ranch and they were hungry again. They could smell good things in the cabin, so they tore off the roof and helped themselves. There was no one to interfere with them so they came back next day to clean up whatever remnants were left. They smashed the stove and stovepipe flat. Evidently one of them thought it a good idea to sit down on the stove.

The cabin had to be repaired and restocked with provisions. By the time the damage was discovered the grizzlies were safe in hibernation, high up on some mountain side and very, very well-fed for their winter sleep.

Bob LaCombe returned in November. When he saw what the bears had done to his house, he went to the Park superintendent. Bob was really mad and got permission to kill any grizzlies that bothered around the ranch in the future.

Like murderers returning to the scenes of their crimes, these bears came back to Buffalo Ranch in April of the following year. By this time the three young ones were almost as large as their mother. She had apparently not been bred for at least three, and more likely four years. They came in the evening just before sun down and when first seen were north of the house on Rose Creek, seeming not in the least afraid. In a few seconds bullets began to fly all around and into them. Two men were shooting as fast as they could work their rifles. The bears just stood and let themselves be shot without making any attempt to get away. The first one fell, and the others gathered around it bewildered. Another was wounded and charged off through the sagebrush until he, too, fell dead. Finally all four of them were stretched out lifeless, four fine animals that had gone berserk. They were criminals, according to man's laws and they paid for their crimes with their lives. They had showed plenty of wit and cunning up to this time and one wonders why they did not run when the firing started. Some of them surely would have escaped.

I skinned them next day. They were the most beautiful bear hides I ever saw. The mother was not an old bear. Her teeth and claws were good and she wore no battle scars around the head as so many grizzlies do.

This is the only instance I know of when bears—either blacks or grizzlies—actually broke into a house for food. Automobiles, yes, by the dozens, and tents and oat boxes—but not dwellings.

It is extremely unusual to find grizzlies in groups of four. During that summer, however, I saw quartets of grizzlies at four different times. There was this group, wiped out by bullets; two groups that were reduced to three each by our bear hunt, and later on a fourth quartet was seen in the central part of the park. It is unlikely that any of these bears were members of two groups.

Bear Facts and Fun

Having had the good fortune to observe various species of bear in their different moods, I am convinced there is as much individuality among bears as among people. Where one will do one thing under a given circumstance, another bear under a similar cirmcumstance will do the opposite. They are cautious and crafty, alert and curious, dignified and playful, as conditions permit or demand. Consequently, one can always expect the unexpected from brother bear.

Our common black and brown bears are considered the clowns of the woods, yet the grizzly, too, has a sense of humor which at times exerts itself in child-like play.

One of the most comical bear shows I ever saw, though it lasted but a few minutes, was put on by a cub on ice. It took place in late April near the junction of the White River and the South Fork of the Flathead River in Montana. At that altitude and time of year, shallow ponds and backwaters were still ice-covered, with broad patches of snow yet remaining on last year's yellow grass.

At the time of the incident, I was looking for two horses that had strayed away from a pack string. I was riding at the edge of a stand of spruce and fir which flanked the spur of a meadow. Upon rounding a point of trees, my horse stopped abruptly, pricked up his ears, and looked across the spur. About two hundred yards away and coming toward me was a brown she-bear and her cub. The cub was a little scamp, and with the old bear stopping every few yards for it to catch up, I felt pretty sure they had just come out of hibernation. Unnoticed, I rode into the timber and stopped to watch them.

An oblong pond, about twenty feet wide and still frozen solid, lay halfway between the horse and me and the bears. It was directly in the route the bears were traveling. A sharply sloping bank, about two feet high, formed the far side of this pond.

Upon reaching the bank, the she-bear stepped down and continued over the ice. The cub, following in her tracks, slipped on the bank and skidded out on the ice a few feet. There it paused in seeming bewilderment. It looked down, pressed its nose to the ice, jerked up its head, then quickly raised one paw and then the other. Suddenly the cub turned and started to dash back to the bank. Its running attempt resulted in a couple of sideway skids and then its paws went out from under it, and it went sprawling. Righting itself, the cub scrambled onto solid ground, abruptly sat down, rolled on its back and began licking the bottom of its paws. It was then I realized the cub's real trouble. The ice had given its tender paws a cold "hot-foot." Soon it arose, moved to the edge of the bank, cocked its fuzzy ears forward, and looked quizzically at the icy pond.

In the meantime, the she-bear had crossed the pond and was standing there watching the cub. Her mouth was open a little way, and with her ears titled forward, her expression was one of mixed understanding and amusement.

Presently the cub looked at her, moved down the bank, started to cross the ice, stepped back, and then started again on the run. Halfway across, the cub's paws went out from under it. The cub went spinning. As it tried to regain its footing, first one paw and then another slipped sideways. Finally the cub remained on its belly and looked around as if taking stock of the situation. Moments later it pushed itself into a sitting position. When its forepaws seemed to be solidly under it, the cub slowly raised its hindquarters until it came to a standing position with its back to its mother. Standing still, the cub turned its head about in a puzzled manner; presenly its nose told it what its eyes didn't see. It looked back over its shoulder and saw its mother. Then, in a very deliberate, slow-motion way, it raised one paw and set it down solidly, then another, and another, as it turned around and moved off the ice.

At its mother's side, the cub sat down and again licked its paws as the she-bear muzzled it soothingly. After a time they turned away and moved up-wind to some nearby timber.

I shall never forget one humorous grizzly digging event I witnessed in the Wyoming Rockies. The wind was blowing toward me as I followed up a little creek. On one side of the stream a log-jam extended out onto a gravel bar. Beyond it a short slope led upward, ending at a line of trees. Halfway up the slope was a three foot bank. As I was rounding a log, a marmot scampered from behind the jam and up the slope to the bank. He dived into a hole leading to his den, and none too soon. A few seconds later a big silver-tip came tearing after him. The bear was about sixty feet away. Thanks to the elements, he had not scented me.

He was moving so fast when his nose went into the hole that his body stopped with an abrupt jar as his head hit the bank. He had seen his quarry enter the hole and evidently thought him trapped, for he began to dig. About a minute later, a movement at the top of the slope caught my eye. About four yards above the bank the marmot came out from behind a clump of grass. He sat on his haunches and looked down at the digging bear. Undoubtedly it was the same one the grizzly had chased into the hole. He had gone through his tunnel home to emerge from his back door. If a marmot could laugh, I am sure this one could have been heard laughing at the bear. Presently the marmot took a shoot of grass in his forepaws and calmly munched it as he watched the grizzly.

By that time, the bear was throwing a steady stream of dirt, small rocks, and clumps of sod out behind him. Several times he paused to sniff in the hole, then dug harder and faster than before. Whenever he dislodged a large rock, he moved it back under him with his forepaw, then he would reach forward with a back leg and cup a hind foot over it, kicking it out and down the slope, never stopping his digging. Nor did he stop when the top of the bank caved in on his head as he undermined it in his forward progress. The bear had been moving earth for about ten minutes when the marmot let go his sharp, characteristic whistle.

Instantly the silver-tip raised his head and looked up the slope above the bank. I'm sure he saw the marmot, for he tensed immediately. Quickly he looked at the hole at his feet, then back at the marmot. I guess the grizzly never thought of a tunnel exit, for he began to dig again quickly. He must have figured the marmot he thought he had cornered in the hole was worth the one on the slope. The marmot ate another shoot of grass before he left his observation post for parts unknown.

By this time the bear had dug a trench three feet wide by about five feet long. From there the grizzly's digging course grew shallower. It moved gradually upward for another seven feet, following the exit tunnel to its end. There the grizzly turned in a circle several times before he sat down. He held his ears a little forward, a bewildered expression on his dirt-covered face, as he looked down the trench he had dug. In all he had been digging about thirty minutes, for nothing.

Hunger sometimes causes a human to do impulsive things, some of which lead to disaster. A demonstration of the same, in the bear family, came to my observation one bright sunny day in 1926.

In the Teton Mountains, near Jackson Hole, Wyoming, I happened to see a brown, she-bear with two fuzzy cubs on a small flat below me. I rode to the lee side of the ridge out of their sight, tied my pack and saddle horses, and hurried back to the ridge top. The bears were still there, unaware of my presence. As the she-bear overturned small boulders in quest of grubs, ants, or mice, the cubs would greedily knock each other about as they dashed under her very nose in an attempt to get any choice morsels she uncovered. The she-bear allowed them to do this several times. Then, in disgust, she sent them sprawling with a quick cuff to get them out of her way.

When almost across the flat, the she-bear came to an alert position and began swinging her head from side to side, testing the wind. Moments later she moved to the base of a barkless snag that stood about ten feet above the ground. She raised up on her hind legs, tilted her head, and looked at the top of the snag. Her tongue lolled out as an expression of clownish-anticipation came over her face. Suddenly she took a few steps forward, placed her forepaws against the snag, and gave it a powerful shove. It went over with the tearing crash of rotted wood, and split open when it hit the ground. The air about the snag instantly became alive with angry bees, for the snag had contained their hive. The she-bear paid no attention to the bees as she gleefully rushed in to get the honey oozing onto the ground. The cubs hesitated only a moment as they cocked their ears forward and looked questioningly at the bees—then they dashed in to join the feast. A split second later they were bawling in fright and pain as they ran back onto the flat amid a cloud of bees.

Squalling and blindly stumbling about, they slapped at their noses, mouths, eyes, and ears with their forepaws in an attempt to fight off the buzzing, stinging horde. To make matters worse, they bumped into each other during their frenzied antics. This, together with their bee trouble, so infuriated them that they unhesitatingly turned upon each other and fought savagely, until distracted by another bee sting. All this kept up until the bees returned to the she-bear who continued eating honey, unmindful of them.

After the bees left, each cub, in an effort to relieve the pain, roughly pawed his swollen nose while rubbing it along the ground. A little later they began casting quick glances from the bees to their mother, while racing back and forth a few yards from her. Their frustrated actions showed they still wanted the sweet, but were afraid to go get it because of the bees. They couldn't seem to understand how the bees stung and hurt them, but not her. They had no way of knowing that the bees could sting through their baby skin, but not her thick, tough hide protected by deep fur and a layer of fat.

When the she-bear had eaten all the honey, she snapped at an antagonistic bee or two, then nonchalantly came over to the cubs. They immediately began licking the honey stuck in the fur on her neck, head, face and paws, as if there had been no bee trouble.

In my estimation, there is no wild animal so comical to watch as a cub bear, especially when it unknowingly mixes inexperience with its comedy.

On a rushing stream in the Sawtooth Mountains of Idaho, I watched a grizzly cub hesitate for some time before following his mother into a swift riffle to fish. Once in the water, he cocked his head as he viewed the fins and tails of salmon darting past him.

196

When one splashed water on him, he jumped backward in curious alarm. When a fish bumped into one of his hind legs, he would spin around in an alert, quizzical manner, and then do the same thing over when bumped again. Presently he sat down in the riffle and watched his mother as she caught and carried two fish out on the bank and ate them. Soon the cub jumped up and bit at a salmon, but it escaped. After several tries, he succeeded in catching a big one. The cub was small and had quite a tussle getting it out on the bank. As he dragged it to where his mother was standing, he tried to raise his forepaws in a prancing fashion, proud of his achievement.

While the bears fished, three crows made their appearance. Each time the she-bear returned to the stream, the crows swooped down to get the salmon remains she had left. The cub took it upon himself to guard the remnants from the crows. Whenever they neared the scraps, he would rise up on his hind legs and bat at them with awkward blows that never quite landed. Sometimes he would fall and land in a wriggling little ball. Then he would clumsily thrash about as he regained his feet for another try.

After several unsuccessful attempts to get at the remains, the crows began to hover a few feet above the cub—just out of reach. This antagonized the little fellow. He crouched, bared his teeth, and jumped at them, only to land in a nose dive with a disgusted snort. Such a procedure happened three times. Each time the crows drew the cub farther away from the scraps. On the cub's next jump, one crow glided quickly behind him and grabbed some fish remnants in its claws. Then it shot upward to the branch of a nearby tree. As soon as the catch was eaten, it rejoined the others in holding the cub's attention, while others grabbed up more scraps.

All the time the crows were harassing the cub, he never sensed the trickery being used to divert his attention from the scraps. When all the remnants were consumed, the crows flew to a snag and began preening themselves in a self-satisfied manner as they watched the cub with a supercilious air.

Scampering to the place where the remains had been, the cub discovered the fish remains were gone. His ears came erect and forward, a blank look appeared on his face as he sniffed about.

Suddenly he half raised up and, with an expression that both questioned and accused, looked over his shoulder at the crows. A moment later he made a mad rush to the snag. When he tried to climb it the crows flew off. The cub sat down on his haunches, shifting his forefeet in a highly agitated manner as he watched the crows disappear from view behind the tree tops.

When a bear decides to run, regardless of looks or size, he is no slouch. He can make a quick getaway, covering ground swiftly. He can move with appalling speed through brush which would hold a man to a crawling pace. I witnessed a bear's hurried run one fall, while hunting deer in the Blue Mountains northeast of Walla Walla, Washington.

I was resting on the edge of a small clearing. To the left was a brush and timber covered hill. Across the clearing before me was a rise of ground covered with a scattered stand of low bushes. A draw, leading to another clearing below, angled along at the edge of another rise to the right. Everything was still. Suddenly the sound of breaking branches came from the left. Within seconds I saw the tops of bushes swaying in the hill, but could not see the cause of the disturbance. Whatever it was, was coming my way full speed ahead. I readied the 30-06. The crashing increased as whatever it was came closer.

Swiftly the brush parted at the edge of the clearing. Out popped a black bear. He looked to be about a year old. He was moving fast. He came right down the center of the clearing in front of me. I thought he was headed for the draw and the country below. In the middle of the clearing, he evidently scented or saw me, although he never looked directly at me. He tried to turn sharply toward the rise of ground across the clearing. His hind feet slid out from under him as his front feet dug into the earth in turning. Amid a shower of dirt, he made several hectic moves to regain his footing, then tore off toward the rise. When he came to it, he made the top in three leaps. He was going so fast his hind feet were up by his ears when his front feet were under and behind him. He was all action, a big, black bottom, with four stems churning for all they were worth.

I spent a good hour trying to find out what started his run. I located the place where he had been ambling along, overturning stones in search of ants and bugs, the spot where he had dug up some bulbs, and beside a log was a mouse nest he had demolished. At that point his tracks ended. They began again eight feet away, where he had started smashing through the brush on his run down the hill. Due to the way the wind was blowing, I felt confident he didn't scent me until he was in the center of the clearing where he made his frantic, wild turn.

One day when fishing on the Cedar River, in Washington, the actions of a well-educated bear, through experience or otherwise, proved that the old saying, "Discretion is the better part of valor," also holds true among wild life.

Fishing hadn't been too good in the river, so I decided to try a small stream that spilled into the river through a narrow, rocky gorge. The water was too swift to ascend in the gorge. I took a nearby trail over a low ridge to get above the narrows. The trail proved to be a long one and upon reaching the ridge top, I sat down on a giant, moss-covered boulder to rest. Seventy feet below me a small marshy area had formed from backwater of the stream. A few yards beyond it the stream thundered into the gorge. Scanning the countryside, I noticed a game trail skirting along a timber stand at the far side of the marsh.

Suddenly I saw a mother skunk and her three little ones moving slowly along a grass-covered, high point of ground that led down the center of the marsh toward the game trail. The little ones were jumping at something their mother carried in her mouth. When the old lady passed an open spot, I saw the object was a wriggling frog.

Just as the skunk family came to the game trail, a yearling cinnamon bear cub (a color phase of the black bear) came abruptly out of the timber onto the trail. The skunks and the bear were less than twenty feet apart when they saw each other. The bear stopped instantly. The odor I expected was not forthcoming. The little skunks hesitated a moment, but their mother never stopped. Threateningly she raised her tail, turned onto the trail, and went directly toward the bear. Her young ones mimicked her every move as they followed her in single file. That bear was wise. He very quickly moved off the trail a good ten feet and sat down facing the skunks.

As the family passed him with arched tails, they turned and held their heads toward him in an "I dare you" attitude. The cub remained motionless and seemingly at attention, for he knew who had the forest right-of-way. When the skunks disappeared around the bend, the bear cautiously came back onto the trail. After looking intently in the direction in which the skunks had disappeared, he moved quietly away in the opposite direction, as if there had been no embarrassing meeting.

We all learn from experience. In the Plumas National Forest, California, I watched a yearling cub learn a lesson from experience in a most unexpected and surprising way.

The cub was as black as ink. It crossed over the creek on a log and scrambled up the bank to a marshy area near a spring. There it prowled about in search of food. Presently it moved up a slope to where several plants were growing. Uprooting one, the cub devoured its bulb-like root, then uprooted another. A few feet away a lone plant, larger than the others, stood out conspicuously. The cub eyed it a moment, then ambled over, uprooted it, and crushed the bulb in its jaws.

Instantly the cub spit out the crushed bulb with a vexed "woof." Backing up in stiff-legged jumps, the cub began spitting and flinging its head from side to side. Suddenly stopping, it placed its nose on the ground and reaching forward with its forepaws, worked at its mouth and nose. After a few seconds of this, the cub dashed to a clear space of water in the marshy area, and thrashed its mouth about in the water. Occasionally the cub stopped and looked up the slope at the mashed bulb with an expression that both questioned and threatened. After a time the cub very cautiously advanced on the bulb, staying within a couple of feet of it, cocking its head a little to one side, and looking questionably at it. Feeling bolder, the cub stretched its neck out and, placing its nose close to the bulb, evidently took a sniff. He jumped back with a noise which was a cross between a sneeze and a woof.

After making a complete circle around the bulb, it moved up the slope. At the top, the cub stopped, looked back at the bulb, swung its head from side to side to test the wind, and then moved out of sight behind some bushes.

Examination showed the mashed bulb to be a wild onion, and from the bear's reactions, a hot one. The other two bulbs were of another plant species, as their leaf structure was of a different kind.

In this modern age, Floyd Barton, who flew over Montana's Flathead Lake country in 1950, 1951, and 1952 for the U. S. Forest Service, told me of seeing grizzlies from the air. While flying low above the trees, he occasionally spotted a grizzly on an open slope or around the lake shore. They would nearly always stand up on their hind legs, turn their heads about in an inquisitive manner, and watch the plane until it became too noisy and close for their comfort. Then they would break and run for cover.

Conclusion

A close analysis of the outlaw grizzly's actions will disclose that all had a somewhat similar pattern of operation, although each developed some individualistic trait. It is rather difficult to understand why they did not change territory, as did the majority of grizzlies, when shot at and continually pursued by stockmen and hunters. Perhaps they were willing to risk the man hazard for a comparatively easy and plentiful fare of domestic stock in an area fast diminishing in wildlife and their natural food supplies.

One must realize that the great majority of grizzlies should not, and cannot, be classified with, or blamed for, the depredations committed by a few of their brothers. When man's encroachment destroyed his natural food supply, he followed the age old instinct for survival and attacked man's livestock. Dr. Bognsong Lekagul, who photographed many grizzlies from 1929 to 1940 for Glacier National Park, says, "I have watched many grizzlies in the wild. I have always found him a true gentleman—except that he was prone to flee if he got my wind (scent). While I have due—and great—respect for his strength, I never was threatened by one, nor was I ever afraid of one. I trust one much, much more than I ever would a black bear that is unpredictable and temperamental."

The professional hunters operating throughout the west in open range days were mostly wise, experienced, old-time trappers. During the summer and sometimes the year round, they were employed by both large and small stockmen to rid their grazing lands of predators. When a mountain lion or grizzly became too troublesome, they concentrated their efforts upon the offender and usually destroyed it before it became a notorious outlaw. Nevertheless, their specialty and chief concern were the wolves, coyotes, and bobcats that gave the stockmen a continuous nightmare.

The first work which could be called the start of the present U. S. Fish and Wildlife Service was set up in economic ornithology by the appropriation act of 1885. The organization became the Division of Biological Survey in 1896 and was made a separate bureau in 1905.

As early as 1905, the U. S. Forest Service employed special predatory animal hunters, but the Biological Survey was co-operating by carrying on investigational work in control methods.

In 1914, U. S. Government hunters took an active part in actual control work through the U. S. Biological Survey, now the U. S. Fish and Wildlife Service, and have continued to this day, together with state hunters in the employ of various state fish and game commissions. Today these hunters wage an unending war on mountain lions, coyotes, and bobcats, which prey on most wildlife and general livestock. The day of the outlaw grizzly, as well as most of the wolves in the states, has long passed.

The professional bear hunters and trappers of days gone by took pelts of thousands of grizzlies, for the grizzly was the prize of the bear family and his hide brought good prices in European and eastern United States markets. I have records of professional bear hunters in Alaska, Canada, and the United States, who took over 100 skins each of these noble animals.

With a horde of such hunters working throughout the west from the middle 1870's, together with the hundreds of grizzlies killed by sportsmen and individual stockmen, it is not difficult to understand why this animal is now near extinction.

During this slaughter, many grizzlies were killed by professional hunters because the animals were blamed for deeds which they did not do.

Today many stockmen, located in big game areas, realize considerable revenue during the hunting season by acting as guides and packers for sportsmen from metropolitan areas. One stockman, operating a two-thousand-acre cow outfit in the foothills of Montana's Absaroka Range, pays his yearly taxes from money received for packing hunting parties to big game haunts. He, and 1200 others throughout the west, are ranchers, besides being registered guides. They, and another 621 men, who operate strictly as guides, are big game's greatest champions for conservation. Laws might not now be so strict had earlier westerners been more reasonable and conservative. It is unfortunate that stockmen of the early days did not have the foresight to realize the value of the grizzly and other species of big game they destroyed so wantonly.

At the present time, only Montana and Wyoming have a limited open season on grizzlies, which, together with the Rocky Mountain bighorn sheep, are the highest prized of all American big game. However, these two states, and others, have open season on other species of big game, which have fared better and are protected by game laws, such as elk, moose, mountain goats, mountain sheep, antelope, the common black, brown, and cinnamon bear, and deer.

The state of Montana has established a large grizzly bear preserve for perpetuation of the species. It is located along the main range of the Rockies, the Continental Divide of the United States, just south of Glacier National Park, in a wild and generally inaccessible region. It is the only sanctuary reserved for protection of grizzlies, other than the U. S. Forests and Parks, within the United States. However, should any grizzly in any protected area wander off and molest livestock, of course, it lays itself open to death at any time.

The end of 1915 saw the grizzly fast nearing extinction with state and federal laws protecting the remaining few. The last outlaw of note, Renegade, was killed in New Mexico in 1915. Yet their legend of strength and fighting ability will live, for the grizzly bear stands as a symbol of many things. The California state flag has a grizzly bear upon it. Indirectly, Yosemite National Park in California was named after the grizzly. "Yosemite" is an Indian word for grizzly. The tribe picked this name, so legend goes, after a valiant fight by a warrior who, single-handedly and unarmed, killed a maddened grizzly on a trail near Yosemite Valley. The Yosemites were a warlike tribe and they were well named after the fighting qualities of the grizzly. The Montana University athletic teams are known as the Montana Grizzlies, while the University of California teams, who use the outline of a grizzly on their insignia, are known as the Golden Bears.

The Smithsonian Institution states that no grizzly population was ever estimated in the early days within the boundary of the United States. Today there are known to be approximately 800 grizzlies throughout this area. The majority of them are now confined to our national parks, forests, and game preserves. From the known thousands in the 1860's, one can estimate how small was the percentage of renegades.

The outlaws mentioned in this book were the most notorious of their time, and all were out and out deliberate livestock slayers. In addition, there were others that carried a reward on their heads, together with a score or so that made spasmodical raids of small significance. The real outlaws were the renegades, the exceptional, the cunning, among their thousands of brothers that lived peacefully throughout the territory which now comprises our western states.

The loss of great numbers of grizzlies will forever be regretted by the sportsmen of the United States and of the world at large.

Although this book deals primarily with notorious grizzlies, I hope, with some statements I have made about grizzlies, I will have helped to correct some common misunderstandings about them, for these great and noble bears had a unique and colorful place in our western history.

1